Mobilizing the Community

to Help Students Succeed

ASCD MEMBER BOOK

Many ASCD members received this book as a
member benefit upon its initial release.

Learn more at: **www.ascd.org/memberbooks**

Mobilizing the Community

to Help Students Succeed

Hugh B. Price

Association for Supervision
and Curriculum Development
Alexandria, Virginia USA

Association for Supervision and Curriculum Development
1703 N. Beauregard St. • Alexandria, VA 22311-1714 USA
Phone: 800-933-2723 or 703-578-9600 • Fax: 703-575-5400
Web site: www.ascd.org • E-mail: member@ascd.org
Author guidelines: www.ascd.org/write

Gene R. Carter, *Executive Director;* Nancy Modrak, *Publisher;* Julie Houtz, *Director of Book
Editing & Production;* Katie Martin, *Project Manager;* Georgia Park, *Senior Graphic Designer;*
BMWW, *Typesetter;* Sarah Plumb, *Production Specialist;* Mike Kalyan, *Production Manager*

Printed in the United States of America. Cover art copyright © 2008 by ASCD. ASCD publica-
tions present a variety of viewpoints. The views expressed or implied in this book should not
be interpreted as official positions of the Association.

All Web links in this book are correct as of the publication date below but may have become
inactive or otherwise modified since that time. If you notice a deactivated or changed link,
please e-mail books@ascd.org with the words "Link Update" in the subject line. In your
message, please specify the Web link, the book title, and the page number on which the link
appears.

ASCD Member Book, No. FY08-8 (July 2008, PS). ASCD Member Books mail to Premium (P)
and Select (S) members on this schedule: Jan., PS; Feb., P; Apr., PS; May, P; July, PS;
Aug., P; Sept., PS; Nov., PS; Dec., P. Select membership was formerly known as
comprehensive membership.

PAPERBACK ISBN: 978-1-4166-0696-3   ASCD product #107055
Also available as an e-book through ebrary, netLibrary, and many online booksellers
(see Books in Print for the ISBNs).

Quantity discounts for the paperback edition only: 10–49 copies, 10%; 50+ copies, 15%; for
1,000 or more copies, call 800-933-2723, ext. 5634, or 703-575-5634. For desk copies:
member@ascd.org.

Library of Congress Cataloging-in-Publication Data

Price, Hugh B.
    Mobilizing the community to help students succeed / Hugh B. Price.
        p. cm.
    Includes bibliographical references and index.
    ISBN 978-1-4166-0696-3 (pbk. : alk. paper)   1. Community and school—United States.
2. Education—Social aspects—United States.   3. Motivation in education—United States—
Citizen participation.   4. Academic achievement—United States.   I. Title.

    LC215.P75 2008
    371.190973—dc22   2008009656

19 18 17 16 15 14 13 12 11 10 09 08   1 2 3 4 5 6 7 8 9 10 11 12

Mobilizing the Community
to Help Students Succeed

Acknowledgments vi

Introduction 1

1. Understanding the Challenge 7

2. Boosting Student Motivation 24

3. Celebrating Student Achievement 44

4. Promoting Academic Success 66

5. Mobilizing the Village 90

Concluding Thoughts 127

References 129

Index 134

About the Author 141

ACKNOWLEDGMENTS

Many colleagues, friends, and family members have contributed importantly to this book. Let me begin by thanking Gene Carter of ASCD for encouraging me to write it. Many thanks also to Scott Willis and Katie Martin of ASCD for helping me to transform my sketchy ideas into a publishable manuscript.

When I headed the National Urban League, and as I wrote this book, I was inspired by the passion and creativity of countless Urban Leaguers, from Velma Cobb, who spearheaded the League's Achievement Campaign, and the late Dr. Israel Tribble, who conceived of the community-based honor society, to the resolute and resourceful Urban Leaguers across the country whose mantra was "Our Children = Our Destiny" and who mobilized their communities to motivate youngsters to achieve.

The Achievement Campaign and this book also owe their existence to many benefactors. The Lilly Endowment and State Farm Life Insurance Companies were steadfast supporters of the Campaign, along with numerous other companies and foundations. The Goldman Sachs Foundation generously underwrote my ability to write this book. The Center on Children and Families at the Brookings Institution provided an intellectually stimulating environment that was perfectly conducive to this project. Oliver W. Sloman, my senior research assistant at Brookings, was an indispensable colleague and dependable reality check.

I owe an unbounded debt of gratitude to my beloved wife, Marilyn, our daughters Traer, Janeen, and Lauren, and our son-in-law Steve Mitchell, who are an enduring source of wisdom and support. Lastly, I am eternally grateful to my nearly 96-year-old mother, Charlotte Price, who never tires of extolling the importance of education.

INTRODUCTION

In the spring of 1994, a lifelong professional dream came true when I was selected as president and CEO of the National Urban League. Founded in 1910 and composed of more than 100 local affiliates across the United States, the Urban League is the oldest and largest community-based movement devoted to empowering black Americans to enter the economic and social mainstream.

Convinced throughout my career that education is key to reaching and remaining in the American mainstream, I was determined to make the promotion of academic achievement the centerpiece of my tenure at the Urban League. I knew that far too many black kids, not to mention other minority and low-income students, were lagging behind academically. And I knew that this so-called achievement gap threatened to hold these children back in school and throughout their lives. But to be truthful, beyond zeroing in on this achievement issue, I didn't yet have a game plan for how the Urban League might leverage its distinctive history and organizational strength to do something about the problem.

When I was in law school, my professors frequently invoked the phrase caveat emptor, which means "buyer beware." In the spirit of that phrase, I should alert readers of this book that I am not a professional educator. Although I have dabbled over the years in teaching seminars at the undergraduate and law school levels, I have never taught in a K–12 classroom, let alone run a school. So my perspectives and recommendations should be read and weighed with that point in mind.

Nevertheless, I am not a stranger to the issues and imperatives facing K–12 education in the United States. As a senior city administrator in New Haven, Connecticut, I spearheaded the substantial expansion of after-school programs in schools and youth services agencies. I once covered education as an editorial writer with the *New York Times*. From 1988 through 1994, I served as vice president of the Rockefeller Foundation, where I helped conceive and launch the National Commission on Teaching and America's Future and the National Guard Youth ChalleNGe Corps, a five-month, quasi-military program aimed at turning around the lives of teenagers who have dropped out of school. On a more personal side, my wife and I are the parents of three daughters, and we interacted extensively with the public schools that educated them. While in law school, I served as a social group worker and mentor for a half-dozen adolescent boys who had frequently been in trouble with the law. Finally, as I'm fond of telling young people in audiences where I'm speaking, I am a "retired kid" with vivid memories of what it was like growing up. Thus, as I embarked on setting the agenda for my administration at the National Urban League, I approached the task, if not as a seasoned educator, from the multiple vantage points of a parent, mentor, journalist, philanthropist, advocate, and (I would like to think) innovator who passionately wants children to succeed in school and schools to succeed by children.

On the eve of my taking office as CEO, a startling article in the *Wall Street Journal* caught my eye. The author, Ron Suskind (1994), describes how high achievers like Cedric Jennings at Ballou High School in Washington, D.C., were so intimidated by their peers that they refrained from attending a school assembly to receive the scholastic honors awards they had earned. Suskind subsequently received a Pulitzer Prize for this riveting story, which he transformed into the acclaimed book *A Hope in the Unseen: An American Odyssey from the Inner City to the Ivy League*. Here is a look at how Suskind describes Cedric's experience:

> On a recent afternoon, a raucous crowd of students fills the gymnasium for an assembly. Administrators here are often forced into bizarre games of cat and mouse with their students, and today is no exception: To lure everyone here, the school has brought in former Washington Mayor Marion Barry, several disc jockeys from a black radio station and a rhythm-and-blues singer.
>
> A major reason for the assembly, though, has been kept a secret: To hand out academic awards to top students. Few of the winners would show up voluntarily to endure the sneers of classmates. When one hapless teen's name is called, a teacher must run to the bleachers and order him down as some in the crowd jeer "Nerd."
>
> The announcer moves on to the next honoree: "Cedric Jennings! Cedric Jennings!" Heads turn expectantly, but Cedric is nowhere to be seen. Someone must have tipped him off, worries Mr. Ballard (the assistant principal). "It sends a terrible message," he says, "that doing well here means you better not show your face."
>
> Cedric, at that moment, is holed up in a chemistry classroom. He often retreats here. It is his private sanctuary, the one

place at Ballou where he feels completely safe, and where he spends hours talking with his mentor. . . . Cedric later will insist he simply didn't know about the assembly—but he readily admits he hid out during a similar assembly last year even though he was supposed to get a $100 prize: "I just couldn't take it, the abuse." (1994, paras. 11–14)

As I read the article, I kept muttering to myself, "This is utterly unacceptable. We just can't have this. We must not let our children turn their backs on academic achievement." Suskind's article was an epiphany because it helped crystallize for me where the Urban League movement might fit into this picture and what it potentially could do about that so-called achievement gap.

Harking back to the famous opening of the hit TV show *Mission: Impossible*, the Urban League's assignment—which I believed we had no choice but to accept—was to mobilize communities to help students succeed. I increasingly became convinced that our job was to galvanize communities to create a pervasive culture of achievement that celebrates and, yes, provides protective cover to achievers, that neutralizes negative peer pressures, and that endeavors to motivate youngsters who scorn academic achievement.

Most of the energy in the contemporary push to improve K–12 schools, boost scholastic performance, and close stubborn achievement gaps is concentrated on accountability and testing, governance and management, curriculum and instruction, strengthened teaching, and school redesign. This is true from the classroom to city hall, from state capitols to the White House. These initiatives unquestionably have merit and appear to be making a positive difference. Yet the persistently poor scholastic performance of far too many youngsters confirms that these measures are not sufficient.

Many a thoughtful article and book has been written about the best ways to improve education and public schools in particular. Numerous experts and observers have weighed in about the obvious importance of parents and caregivers, and I certainly said my piece on this subject in my book *Achievement Matters: Getting Your Child the Best Education Possible* (Price, 2002). What's surprising, though, is how little attention has been paid to the responsibility and potential role of the community in fostering academic achievement. Instinct, experience, observation, and research all convince me that these wider social structures can play an indispensable part in promoting literacy and achievement.

This book is written for educators who wish to mobilize their own communities to support student success. It addresses an important gap in the multifaceted strategy that school superintendents, principals, education leaders, and practitioners should pursue in partnership with community groups to maximize their chance of boosting student achievement, especially among those young people who tend to be the hardest to reach and teach. My aim is to provide vivid illustrations of what can be done based on what has actually been done and to share other promising ideas worth trying. I also hope to pass on concrete, real-world tips for implementing a community mobilization effort.

Because my own professional expertise and the examples I cite are rooted in the U.S. experience and, even more specifically, in the experience of minority-majority urban schools, this book will resonate most obviously with U.S. audiences. Yet the fundamental message is not confined by ethnicity or economic status, much less by oceans or national boundaries. Nations around the world contain cities and rural regions with high concentrations of underachieving and unmotivated young people who are at risk of losing hope. It is *my* hope that this book will prove helpful to educators and community leaders who are determined to boost these youngsters' academic performance and life prospects.

During 2006–2007, I proudly served as cochair of the Commission on the Whole Child. It was established by the Association for Supervision and Curriculum Development (ASCD) out of the firm conviction that the success of each learner can be achieved only through a whole child approach, and that teachers, schools, and communities need to forge a new compact based on shared responsibility for the effective education and healthy development of children. The Commission's report, *The Learning Compact Redefined* (ASCD, 2007), calls on communities to provide

- Family support and involvement;
- Government, civic, and business support and resources;
- Volunteers and advocates; and
- Support for their districts' coordinated school health councils or other collaborative structures (p. 3).

With this book I want, in poker parlance, to call and raise the Commission's recommendations. The real-world experiences captured in this book convince me that well-organized communities working in sync with schools and educators can do even more to stoke students' desire for achievement. A thoughtfully designed and faithfully executed campaign to motivate youngsters to succeed in school creates a "win–win–win," for educators, for students, and for entire nations— present and future.

1

UNDERSTANDING
THE CHALLENGE

In May 2007, the U.S. Department of Education and the Census Bureau issued a study indicating that minority students have surged to 42 percent of public school enrollment nationally (Dillon, 2007). That's up from 22 percent just three decades ago and is primarily attributable to robust growth in the Latino population. A pressing challenge for U.S. schools—and for the nation as a whole—arises from the fact that these students, along with low-income youngsters, consistently lag behind academically.

The National Assessment of Educational Progress (NAEP) is often referred to as the "nation's report card." Although some scholars argue that NAEP has flaws (see, for example, Loveless, 2006), it remains the only gauge of K–12 student achievement across states. The subject-specific exams, which sample student achievement instead of testing every student, posit three levels of academic competence:

- *Basic*. This level denotes partial mastery of prerequisite knowledge and skills that are fundamental for proficient work at each grade.
- *Proficient*. This level represents solid academic performance for each grade assessed. Students reaching this level have

demonstrated competency over challenging subject matter, including subject-matter knowledge, application of such knowledge to real world situations, and analytical skills appropriate to the subject matter.

• *Advanced.* This level signifies superior performance. (National Assessment Governing Board, n.d., para. 2)

In actuality, NAEP has an unofficial fourth level of achievement: "Below Basic." As the figure on page 9 shows, a dismayingly high proportion of U.S. youngsters have languished at the "Below Basic" performance level for many years.

The imperative of boosting youngsters from Below Basic to Basic and beyond transcends race and ethnicity. Even though the ratios of low-achieving youngsters are most pronounced among black, Latino, and American Indian students, white students far outnumber those from other ethnic groups, and, according to NAEP, during the 1990s they constituted 37.6 percent of all youngsters scoring in the lowest quintile compared with 32.8 percent of black students and 29.6 percent of Latino students (Flanagan & Grissmer, 2002).

The Preparation Gap

Not surprisingly, the sizeable skills gap reflected by NAEP creates a preparation gap for low achievers. By "preparation gap," I mean the difference between what youngsters know and are able to do and what they need to know and be able to do to succeed in school, function effectively in postsecondary education, land a job with good pay and benefits, and go on to enjoy a middle-class lifestyle. According to Charles Kolb (2006), CEO of the Committee for Economic Development, in the United States only 20 percent of black students and

NAEP Results for 4th and 8th Graders in Mathematics and Reading, 1992–2007

Group	Percent Scoring Below Basic			
	1992	2000	2005	2007
Hispanic				
4th grade reading	61	63	54	50
8th grade reading	51	—	44	42
4th grade math	66	58	32	30
8th grade math	65	59	48	45
African American				
4th grade reading	68	65	58	54
8th grade reading	55	45	48	45
4th grade math	78	64	40	36
8th grade math	80	69	58	53
American Indian				
4th grade reading	—	—	52	51
8th grade reading	—	—	41	44
4th grade math	—	—	32	30
8th grade math	—	—	47	47
Eligible for free/reduced-price lunch				
4th grade reading	—	62	54	50
8th grade reading	—	—	43	42
4th grade math	—	57	33	30
8th grade math	—	—	49	45
White				
4th grade reading	29	30	24	22
8th grade reading	23	—	18	16
4th grade math	31	22	10	9
8th grade math	32	24	20	18
Asian/Pacific Islander				
4th grade reading	40	30	27	23
8th grade reading	24	—	20	20
4th grade math	27	—	10	9
8th grade math	24	25	19	17

Source: National Center for Education Statistics, "2007 NAEP Results: Results by Demographic Group," retrieved September 2007 from http://nces.ed.gov/nationsreportcard/

16 percent of Latino students graduate from high school adequately prepared for college.

The Dropout Crisis

The picture becomes grimmer still when we consider that large numbers of black and Latino high school students do not graduate at all. According to "Diplomas Count" (2006), a special supplement issued by *Education Week*, just half of black students and roughly 55 percent of Latino students graduate from high school, contrasted with more than three-quarters of non-Hispanic white and Asian students. Some scholars, like Lawrence Mishel (2006) of the Economic Policy Institute, contend that dropout rates this high are exaggerated; his analysis concludes that 73 percent of black students graduate on time. But whether the dropout rate for black students is Mishel's 27 percent, twice that, or somewhere in between, what cannot be disputed is that the dropout crisis is concentrated ethnically, socioeconomically, and geographically—and it's getting worse.

According to Robert Balfanz and Nettie Legters (2006) of Johns Hopkins University, nearly half of the nation's Latino and black students attend high schools with high poverty rates and low graduation rates. Roughly 15 percent of U.S. high schools produce close to half of the nation's dropouts. Balfanz and Legters brand these 2,000 dysfunctional high schools "dropout factories" (p. 42). They report that many of the students who attend these so-called dropout factories enter high school poorly prepared for academic success and rarely (or barely) make it out of the 9th grade. Typically these students stop focusing in class, attend infrequently, fail too many courses to be promoted to the 10th grade, try again with no better results, and ultimately drop out. Twenty to 40 percent repeat the 9th grade, but only 10 to 15 percent of "repeaters" go on to graduate.

It's interesting that in a series of focus groups conducted in 2005 with dropouts in Philadelphia and Baltimore, few of these youngsters cited academic struggles as their primary reason for dropping out. They were far more likely to say they left school because they were unmotivated, were not challenged enough, or were overwhelmed by troubles outside school (Gewertz, 2006).

The Disengagement Crisis

The phenomenon of student disengagement is less documented and publicized than the dropout crisis but no less ominous. I refer here to youngsters who lose interest in school and virtually give up trying to learn, achieve, and acquire essential skills, even though they technically remain enrolled. Standing on the precipice of dropping out, these students face lengthening odds that they'll ever graduate and go on to postsecondary education.

In the view of Eddy Bayardelle, president of the Merrill Lynch Foundation and a former teacher and principal in the New York City school system, schools are filled with children who have simply tuned out. He contends that school systems do not know what to do with these students, traditional schools do not reach them, and the kids themselves do not particularly care about remaining unreached. As he told me, they simply aren't "into" the education that's being offered.

The Higher Education Gap

Achievement deficits shadow young people after high school. In Washington, D.C., for instance, a study commissioned by city and school officials reports that only nine percent of 9th graders in the public schools will complete college within five years of graduating from high school (Haynes, 1996). The report further asserts that

9 out of 10 freshmen in D.C. public schools could expect to be confined to low-paying jobs because they will never begin college or will fail to complete it.

As Tamar Lewin (2006) reports in the *New York Times* on a study by the National Center for Public Policy and Higher Education, "The United States, long the world leader in higher education, has fallen behind other nations in its college enrollment and completion rates" (p. A23). Although the United States still ranks first in the proportion of 35- to 64-year-olds with college degrees, it has fallen to seventh place among developed nations in the proportion of 25- to 34-year-olds with college degrees (Lewin, 2006). According to one study, the share of the U.S. workforce with high school and college degrees may even decline slightly over the next 15 years, as highly educated baby boomers retire and are replaced by young Latino and black workers—who, if current patterns persist, are far less likely to earn high school and college degrees.

The bottom line is that low matriculation and graduation rates, fueled significantly by K–12 achievement and preparation gaps, threaten U.S. productivity and competitiveness. And because workers with fewer years of education earn so much less, living standards in the United States could plunge unless something is done to close these achievement gaps, especially among black, Latino, and low-income youngsters (Symonds, 2005).

The State of School Reform

No Child Left Behind (NCLB), the federal law enacted in 2001, mandated new testing, accountability, and transparency measures for U.S. public schools. This audacious legislation also decreed that by the end of the 2006 school year every core-subject classroom will be led by a "highly qualified teacher" and, furthermore, that by 2014 all students will be proficient in reading and mathematics. The first target has already been missed by a wide margin. Meeting the latter target is highly doubtful.

In addition to NCLB, a potpourri of other, mostly unsynchronized federal, state, and local initiatives has focused in recent years on a litany of school reforms: imposing tougher high school graduation standards, establishing high-stakes tests as prerequisites for advancing from grade to grade, ending social promotion, revising state school aid formulas, downsizing schools and reducing class sizes, creating career academies and other schools-within-schools, reforming curricula, expanding quality preschool programs, launching charter schools and other variations of autonomous schools, upgrading the caliber of teachers, and asserting mayoral control over school systems. What have these attempts at reform wrought when it comes to school effectiveness and student achievement?

On the upside, the campaign to improve public education has continued when it might easily have petered out. That persistence is a testament both to the resolve of successive waves of dedicated educators and determined reformers and to the collective realization among policymakers and employers that the stakes for our society and economy are too high to retreat short of significant progress. No Child Left Behind has provoked closer media scrutiny of school performance and has heightened parental awareness of how their children are faring. The law also sheds useful light on how well individual schools are serving various categories of students, especially chronic underachievers, and in this way, it has unquestionably ratcheted up the pressure on public schools to perform.

The verdict on education reform's effect on student performance is murkier, however. Although some public school systems are beginning to register credible and encouraging academic gains, these gains fall short of a grade of "satisfactory progress." As Lynn Olson (2006) writes in *Education Week*:

> It would be hard to ignore the fact that progress has not come nearly far or fast enough. That's particularly true in reading, where average scores nationally have barely budged since 1992. It's also true that, despite the solid gains of poor, African-American, and Hispanic students during this period, the achievement gaps between those students and their more affluent and white peers remain disturbingly deep—at least 20 points in both grades and subjects (reading and math), or the equivalent of two grade levels or more. . . . After widening a bit during the mid-1990s, those gaps have begun to close again. But in many cases, the gaps now mirror what they were in the early '90s, and progress in closing them has been less dramatic since 2003. (pp. 9–10)

Current school reform measures will likely continue to support incremental progress, with only modest annual improvements. The reason for this is that the pressure to achieve is trained on teachers and on children, many of whom are already achievement inclined. It isn't clear that higher standards and accountability pressure are having a positive influence on the bulk of struggling students who continue to perform poorly in school year after year.

Finding Support Beyond the Schoolhouse

It's time to realize that when it comes to educating youngsters who struggle in school, educators cannot succeed on their own. In order to accelerate the pace of improvement in large populations of youngsters who chronically perform below par, we must augment the accountability and reform initiatives currently focused on school systems and schools with initiatives aimed at stoking *a heightened desire for achievement* on the part of these children, their families, and community groups. In short, what's missing from the school reform playbook is an emphasis on motivation: sustained and effective encouragement for these underachievers to succeed. And conspicuously missing from teams of reformers that must figure out how to do this is the community—the proverbial village, in its myriad organizational forms.

Parental Involvement

Much has been written about the vitally important role of parents and caring adults in encouraging their children to achieve. I've contributed to the literature on this topic with my 2002 book, *Achievement Matters: Getting Your Child the Best Education Possible.* Anyone who has raised a child knows firsthand what a difference he or she can make in motivating a youngster. Inspiring examples abound of parents stepping up their efforts on this front. For example, the *Washington Post* carried a front-page story on a determined effort by 15 black families in Loudoun County, Virginia, to keep their teenaged sons academically engaged (Chandler, 2007). The boys belong to Club 2012, so named because the objective is to make certain they graduate from high school on schedule in 2012. The group holds monthly meetings, conducts homework sessions twice a week, and engages fathers and sons in ongoing conversation.

My family lives in an economically and ethnically diverse community in Westchester County, New York, where active (bordering on overbearing) parent involvement in the schools is the norm. This involvement clearly shows in the way children achieve and in how attentive the schools are to the needs of youngsters whose parents are actively engaged. The combination of students who want to achieve and parents who are intent on them achieving is potent, and it produces results.

As beneficial as parent involvement in school can be, the reality is that many parents do not become involved, and those who might be inclined to get involved may not know how to do so. Minority and low-income parents are often less involved in their children's education than families who are better off economically (Hill et al., 2004). While touring the United States in support of my book *Achievement Matters*, I spoke with many who were unsure why they needed to be involved anyway. "Why can't I just trust the teachers?" they asked me. To my mind, this question is a proxy for other, unexpressed sentiments. Some of these parents may not have the time, interest, or energy to get involved, and it's unclear whether they will be an insistent and consistent force in encouraging their children to achieve. Or, perhaps, having themselves had a negative experience in school, they lack the requisite confidence, knowledge, or skills to make their children's experience positive. As Yale University's James P. Comer (2004) observes,

> Many of today's students at greatest risk for underachievement or school failure are growing up in families that did not experience three generations of acculturation and upward mobility. . . . Most often both parents, or the single parent, are in the workforce with low-paying jobs. The parents want their children to be successful in school and in life, but they themselves have not had the experience they need to help their children do so. (p. 89)

Moreover, parental involvement in school often declines during adolescence (Hill et al., 2004), the point at which older children are becoming more assertive and seeking greater autonomy from their families. As parental influence recedes, these youngsters turn to their peers and larger social structures around them. This is all the more reason why communities must get involved in promoting achievement.

Community Involvement

Research and common sense substantiate the importance of active community involvement in children's education. (That's certainly consistent with my own experience, first as a pupil eons ago and subsequently as a parent.) Communities should motivate youngsters to take school seriously and strive to achieve, and should celebrate them when they do. This culture of achievement augments the efforts of engaged parents and helps fill the void created by parents who are not involved.

Let me explain more fully what I mean by that all-too-familiar term *community*. To me, and for the purposes of this book, community runs the gamut of volunteer civic and social groups; sororities and fraternities; block clubs; parent–teacher groups; churches and faith-based organizations; settlement houses; community centers; and youth-serving agencies like Boys and Girls Clubs, the YMCA, and the YWCA. It also encompasses civic-oriented groups like the Kiwanis and Lions, Head Start centers, advocacy groups, social service agencies, and other community-based organizations (CBOs) like the local Urban League. A common denominator in my definition of community organizations is that these are not government entities, even though some of them may receive public funding. Civic-minded entrepreneurs and business groups fit the bill as well. Some nonprofit groups that help make up the community are professionally staffed and provide services week in and week out. Others are essentially volunteer organizations whose members meet weekly or monthly.

The Importance of Community Norms

Research tells us that expectations, mores, values, and norms set by communities can affect student motivation. As James Coleman (1988) of the University of Chicago writes, "When a norm exists and is effective, it constitutes a powerful, though sometimes fragile, form of social capital. . . . Norms in a community that support and provide effective rewards for high achievement in school greatly facilitate the school's task" (p. S104). Norms aren't the sole province of parents, Coleman argues. Based on his research, he concludes,

> The social capital that has value for a young person's development does not reside solely within the family. It can be found outside as well in the community consisting of the social relationships that exist among parents, in the closure exhibited by this structure of relations, and in the parents' relations with the institutions of the community. (p. S113)

Coleman explains that in an examination of parochial schools, he found that community norms played a discernible role in the way students behaved in school: "The low dropout rates of the Catholic schools, the low dropout rates in the other private schools, and the independent effect of frequency of religious attendance all provide evidence of the importance of social capital outside the school, in the adult community surrounding it, for this outcome of education" (p. S115).

Children do indeed pay attention to values and norms transmitted by others. Researchers generally agree that children develop a self-concept primarily through their interpretations of the reflected appraisals of others (Aronson, 2002). Because young children aren't yet adept at self-appraisal, they tend to rely on others' opinions to create their own judgments of confidence and self-worth. And because youngsters validate their identity through the evaluations of significant others, family members, teachers, and even trusted members of the community influence the development of a positive self-image. Absent these social structures, children seek validation elsewhere, too often with disastrous results. I am reminded of this statement from a Chicago gang leader, quoted by Kunjufu (1988): "We will always have the youth, because we make them feel important" (p. 86).

Black Student Achievement: A Case in Point

Community norms have traditionally played a particularly central role in the lives of black Americans. Comer (2004) observes that

> The church and community-based culture of African-Americans, while still marginal to the mainstream, served important protective and promotive functions. It provided many with a sense of adequacy and belonging. . . . The church- and community-based culture provided belief and behavior systems that made desirable social and family functioning and achievement possible. (p. 87)

Comer (2004) focuses on the ways this scenario has played out in black history, noting that in the 1960s, before many families were prepared to benefit from new opportunities, high mobility and mass communication began to cause a breakdown in community and family life across the racial, ethnic, and income spectra. Prior to the weakening of protective and promotive cultural structures among blacks, many families used these structures to create beliefs and values, and to gain direction in their own lives. Comer argues that the once-powerful positive effects of well-functioning and church-based cultures have been diminished by the breakdown in community and the powerful effects of mainstream media entertainment that glorifies often harmful habits and styles that are distinctly not mainstream. Geoffrey Canada, founder of the Harlem Children's Zone, puts it bluntly: "The real values that have been the bedrock of the African-American community get drowned out by a variety of forces" (Poindexter, 2001, p. 6). Canada goes on to say that educators, parents, and community activists "need to set up a counter-culture that pushes the values we are about—hard work, academic achievement, sobriety, honesty" (p. 6).

It's up to the community to set these values and to do so in ways that are synchronized with and supportive of what is happening in the classroom. In his research, Ogbu (1992) affirms the constructive role of community in encouraging achievement among academically successful minority groups. "The community," he observes, ". . . appears to use both tangible and symbolic means to encourage school striving" (p. 11). He also notes that

> The meaning and value students associate with school learning and achievement play a very significant role in determining their efforts toward learning and performance. Furthermore, the meaning and value that students from different cultural groups associate with the process of formal education vary and are socially transmitted by their ethnic communities. (p. 7)

Ogbu recommends several ways that minority communities can encourage academic striving and success among their children, including providing youngsters with "concrete evidence that its members appreciate and value academic success as much as they appreciate and value achievements in sports, athletics and entertainment" (1992, p. 12). In this way, communities can reassert the vitally important normative and proselytizing role that Comer argues they once played in steering young people along the path of education toward the American mainstream.

Unleashing Community Energy

If communities are aggressively mobilized and their energies are productively focused, they can transmit pro-achievement values to counteract student negativity toward and disengagement with school.

From my daughter's and my own experiences as volunteer mentors, I can attest that something as simple as community mentoring can turn underachievers on to school. That's why after-school programs—whether run by schools, churches, or community-based organizations—are vitally important. However, the sheer scale of the underachievement phenomenon far exceeds the scope and capacity of these mentoring programs. There isn't remotely enough money in the public or philanthropic sectors to set up one-on-one mentoring for all the children who need it. And so there is a pressing need for large-scale strategies to transform the attitudes and aspirations of these youngsters toward school and to spur families and CBOs to spread the gospel of achievement—a message that's far too important to be vulnerable to the vicissitudes of external funding.

For all their potential as valuable players in the school reform arena, communities remain a largely underappreciated and untapped resource. Perhaps this is because mobilizing them isn't a sure or easy thing. The question that school superintendents and other educators would profit from addressing—and answering—is how best to galvanize and deploy volunteer energy in ways that are constructive and productive. When community groups want to pitch in, what strategies will best capitalize on their assets so that their involvement produces better outcomes for schoolchildren as opposed to busy-work, distractions, and tension for school personnel? What can educators do to first galvanize and then direct community energy in ways that complement what is going on in the classroom?

I realize that some educators are wary when it comes to reaching out to noneducators, much less collaborating with them. Even administrators and teachers who are willing to take this step may not know how to enlist the help of community groups and sustain harmonious partnerships. However, the sheer stubbornness and pervasiveness of the underachievement phenomenon dictate that educators and community groups venture beyond their respective comfort zones and forge new collaborations based on their shared stake in boosting student achievement.

Educators can learn from the ways that the National Urban League and its affiliates went about mobilizing their communities to help students succeed. Educators can apply some of the tactics that the Urban League used to reach out to other community organizations and craft plans to boost student motivation, celebrate student achievement, and promote academic success. These examples may also inspire educators to come up with other mobilization ideas that are even better suited to the unique circumstances of their communities.

My main message is this: While our Achievement Campaign didn't always meet my stratospheric expectations, it never backfired on us. Done hastily and clumsily, community mobilization can sputter and disappoint. Done well, the potential benefits for children and their schools are considerable.

The Challenge We Face

- Wide achievement gaps and high dropout rates persist despite intensive school reform efforts; these deficits threaten children's futures and our nation's quality of life.
- Disengaged students pose serious challenges for educators, parents, and communities.
- Modernity has weakened community influence, yet communities still set expectations and values that actually influence kids.
- Motivating students is missing from the school-reform playbook.
- Educators must reach out to communities, an underused ally capable of fostering a culture of achievement.

2

BOOSTING STUDENT MOTIVATION

Although the issue of student motivation receives scant attention from proponents of testing and tough love, the truth (at least according to many researchers) is that student motivation really does matter. So do its conceptual siblings: conscientiousness, self-confidence, self-discipline, and responsibility. Children begin life ready and willing to learn. But as they progress through the primary grades, a great many lose their natural curiosity and enthusiasm for learning. Rekindling this enthusiasm is one of the keys to improving student achievement, and the community has an essential role to play in that effort.

Research on Motivation

Persuasive links between lack of motivation and low achievement have been uncovered by a variety of researchers, including Geoffrey Schultz of Indiana University; Franzis Preckel of the University of Munich; Ericka Fisher of Holy Cross College; Donna Ford of Peabody College at Vanderbilt; Roslyn Arlin Mickelson of the University of North Carolina at Charlotte; and the late John Ogbu, the noted anthropologist. Studies of minority children generally indicate that those who are more motivated to achieve perform better academically than those who are less motivated (Schultz, 1993). Why is this so? Research suggests that students who believe they will be successful engage in more metacognition, use more effective cognitive strategies, persist on tasks longer, expend more effort, and, therefore, perform better academically than those who are less motivated and confident (Schultz, 1993).

Conscientiousness is a personality trait closely related to motivation and thus relevant to academic achievement as well. Several studies have shown that conscientiousness is a valid predictor for academic success (Preckel, Holling, & Vock, 2006). After all, it stands to reason that young people who are very conscientious—who are disciplined and dutiful—can fulfill the demands of school more easily.

Still other researchers cite confidence as a key contributor to academic success. According to Fisher (2005), the academic success of high achievers appears to be a direct result of several factors: high self-concepts, time management skills, parental support and high expectations, the desire to prove stereotypes wrong, their own high expectations, and the desire to be responsible for their own lives and control their own destiny.

In the same study, low achievers viewed themselves as smart but lazy. They were fully aware that with effort they would achieve greater academic success (Fisher, 2005). They often felt as if they were "just 1 of 20" and that they received little if any individual support or encouragement. These low achievers also believed that most of their teachers had prejudged them before getting to know them as students. This perceived lack of support and connection to the school, combined with parental tolerance of mediocre grades, contributed to low academic performance, in these youngsters' view.

Because students are human beings, the explanation of what motivates them and why isn't always logical or straightforward, especially from an adult perspective. Some underachievers acknowledge that it is cool to be smart. Even so, they may be lured by financial opportunities and emotional imperatives that aren't dependent on schooling. Underachievers who see the world this way claim that their lack of academic success isn't the result of embracing a so-called oppositional culture or, in the case of black kids, rejecting achievement as "acting white." Rather, they say they are coping with rejection in school by pursuing other routes to economic success, such as entertainment or professional sports (Fisher, 2005).

Not surprisingly, socioeconomic status also bears on motivation. Schultz (1993) suggests that minority children with greater socioeconomic advantages typically perform better in school than less-advantaged students. Interestingly enough, the differences become particularly dramatic after the 3rd grade and appear to have no correlation with children's intellectual abilities.

Perceptions of opportunity and obstacles also appear to shape student motivation. Scholars like Ogbu, for instance, have suggested that black students perceive the opportunity structure more negatively than do white students. They are less confident that hard work, effort, and academic success will produce occupational and economic rewards commensurate with their educational credentials. This skepticism causes some kids to become disillusioned with the value of schooling. They may even view school as forcing them to sacrifice their sense of identity to succeed academically (Ford & Harris, 1996).

As if that isn't complication enough, when it comes to motivation, the need to belong and allegiance to peers often take precedence in the lives of many students. For example, students who feel alienated from, unaccepted by, and unconnected to their peers may become introverted, withdrawn, aggressive, or disruptive. This reaction can take a psychological toll on their motivation and attitudes because of the conflict between the expectation to achieve and their need for affiliation and belonging (Ford & Harris, 1996).

A worrisome deficit of motivation surfaces especially among low-income and minority youngsters. The explanations for these counterproductive attitudes run the gamut from the chilling effects of socioeconomic disadvantage, to the related inability to see a connection between academic achievement and opportunity for success in life, to an embrace of so-called oppositional cultures that reject achievement. As Mickelson (1990) once observed, "Working-class and minority youths have parents, older siblings, and neighbors whose real-world experiences challenge the myth that education equals opportunity for all" (p. 59).

Clearly, then, students' motivation and mind-set toward academic achievement can affect how well they'll do in school. In the absence of ingrained motivation or familial influences, education can be a steep uphill climb for some students.

Fortunately, lack of motivation is reversible. Although browbeating disinterested and slacking students to "try harder" isn't a very effective technique and may even increase alienation from school, motivation *can* be inculcated, cultivated and unleashed, nurtured and ignited. Youngsters can be influenced by their parents, teachers, relatives, and mentors. As we will see, students also are susceptible and responsive to encouragement from other individuals and organizations rooted in their communities.

The idea behind motivating kids to achieve isn't necessarily to try to transform all of them into Phi Beta Kappas and Rhodes Scholars (although that would be fine, of course). Rather, the point is to get them to strive to do well in school so that, at a minimum, they achieve up to their potential, become academically proficient, and emerge from school prepared for self-reliance and citizenship in a world where so-called knowledge workers live far more comfortably than unskilled laborers.

Insights from the Military

Although it's probably unusual for K–12 educators to look to the military for insights and models, the truth is that the military knows a lot about motivating, training, and developing young people that might be applicable in public school settings. (In fact, I wrote a paper for the Brookings Institution on this very topic; see Price, 2007.) For instance, the strict discipline long associated with military training helps instill the motivation that may be in short supply among some young people. As the Center for Strategic and International Studies (CSIS) states in its report entitled *Forging a Military Youth Corps: A Military–Youth Service Partnership for High School Dropouts*:

> Those who train military recruits . . . along with any experienced parents, will attest that discipline is part of what young people need most. It appears in many forms, whether it makes an athlete rise at dawn to train, drives a writer to spend personal time finishing a chapter, or motivates a military recruit to follow a squad leader's instructions. . . . Self-discipline, a significant factor of maturity, is what allows parents, tired from a day's work, to still care for a home and children, and it is what makes them go to work in the first place. (Cullinan, Eaves, McCurdy, & McCain, 1992, pp. 6–7)

Several public school districts, like those in Chicago, Philadelphia, and Maryland's Prince George's County, have created high schools that mirror some attributes of the military. In the words of Phyllis Goodson, principal of the Chicago Military Academy–Bronzeville, "Military is the culture we follow; we say 'Yes sir' and 'No ma'am.' But we're not seeking outward control or manipulation of our students. We're taking dependent children and teaching them self-discipline, self-control, and confidence" (McCarthy, 2003, p. A1).

Interestingly enough, for all the shouting and belittling that traditionally characterize basic training, the military actually excels at valuing and challenging young people and believes in the potential of every recruit and cadet. Indeed, that perspective characterizes the essence of the way it operates.

Ways to Motivate Students

Over the years, efforts to boost student achievement have tended to focus, for understandable reasons, on complex and politically contentious reforms in testing and accountability, governance, and instruction. Yet the field of social psychology has much to offer as well. Positive changes in student motivation can produce gains in students' academic achievement. As Dweck (2002) observes,

> It is sometimes surprising to those who are not social psychologists that what look like minor belief-changing interventions—teaching students a different view of intelligence, teaching them a different interpretation for failure, or orienting them toward different reasons for achieving—end up having real effects on students' school engagement and achievement. . . . They are used to seeing hugely expensive, large-scale, long-term, multifaceted interventions yield only small effects. Yet, social psychologists understand the power of a carefully targeted intervention

that changes a key belief and refocuses students' motivation in highly productive ways. (p. 41)

Value Students as Individuals

Another subtle yet essential issue that affects whether children are motivated to achieve is whether they feel valued or devalued. Claude Steele (1992), a social psychologist at Stanford University who studies achievement among black children, characterizes this starkly as

> a culprit that can undermine black achievement as effectively as a lock on a schoolhouse door. The culprit I see is stigma, the endemic devaluation many blacks face in our society and schools. This status is its own condition of life, different from class, money, culture. . . . [I]ts connection to school achievement among black Americans has been vastly underappreciated. (para. 4)

Other low-income and minority youngsters, children with attention deficit disorder, and special education students who tend to struggle in school are susceptible to being underappreciated by their teachers. "Doing well in school requires a belief that school achievement can be a promising basis for self-esteem," Steele argues, "and that belief needs constant reaffirmation even for advantaged students" (1992, para. 17). In his view, children who are devalued academically may "disidentify" with doing well in school.

As illustration, Steele cites the inspiring work of Uri Treisman, a professor of mathematics at the University of Texas at Austin. Treisman recruited black youngsters who were performing poorly in math into his Mathematics Workshop Program. In surprisingly short order, their grades soared, even to the point of outperforming white and

Asian counterparts. According to Steele, Treisman's message to the former underachievers was, in effect, "You are valued in this program because of your academic potential—regardless of your current skill level. You have no more to fear than the next person, and since the work is difficult, success is a credit to your ability, and a setback is a reflection only of the challenge" (1992, para. 34).

In Steele's view, "Psychology is everything: remediation defeats, challenge strengthens—affirming their potential, crediting them with their achievements, inspiring them" (1992, para. 46). The key, he argues, is ensuring that youngsters who are vulnerable on so many counts get treated essentially like middle-class students, with conviction about their value and promise. As this happens, their vulnerability diminishes, and with it the companion defense of "disidentification" and misconduct. As Steele puts it, "Where students are valued and challenged, they generally succeed" (para. 47).

Whether parents realize it or not, they can value (or devalue) their children by the way they converse with them. Two child psychologists, Betty Hart and Todd R. Risley, studied verbal exchanges between parents and children. According to an article about this study in the *New York Times Magazine*, the researchers found that

> The kinds of words and statements that children heard varied by (economic) class. The most basic difference was in the number of "discouragements" a child heard—prohibitions and words of disapproval—compared with the number of encouragements, or words of praise and approval. By age 3, the average child of a professional heard about 500,000 encouragements and 80,000 discouragements. For the welfare children, the situation was reversed: they heard, on average, about 75,000 encouragements and 200,000 discouragements. Hart and Risely found

that as the number of words a child heard moved beyond simple instructions, it blossomed into discussion of the past and future, of feelings, of abstractions, of the way one thing causes another—all of which stimulated intellectual development. (Tough, 2006, p. 48)

Consistent discouragement, which is tantamount to devaluation in my view, can harm intellectual development and achievement. The article continues:

Hart and Risley showed that language exposure in early childhood correlated strongly with I.Q. and academic success later on in a child's life. Hearing fewer words, and a lot of prohibitions and discouragements, had a negative effect on I.Q.; hearing lots of words, and more affirmations and complex sentences, had a positive effect on I.Q. The professional parents were giving their children an advantage with every word they spoke, and the advantage just kept building up. (Tough, 2006, p. 48)

The importance to youngsters of being valued apparently increases as they enter adolescence. As Venable (1997) observes, before adolescent children can reach adulthood, they need to be valued and have a clear role and status as a person who counts. Yet when adolescents handle their own transition into adulthood, the results can be destructive. If children are not valued at home or by significant adults, they will find a peer group or gang that approves of them. In Venable's view, adolescents who are not given the opportunity to share the status of responsible and competent adults may develop illegal, immoral, or near-fatal "initiation rites into their own ignored adolescent culture. Having adult status denied them, many teenagers in the crucible of adolescence have sought ingenuous, and often-times damaging, means of attaining that status" (p. 7).

When I was growing up in Washington, D.C., I experienced a form of devaluation that rattled my self-confidence. During the summer between my junior and senior years in high school, I was selected to participate in a summer employment program for students who were very strong in math and science. For some reason, our employer, a Defense Department subcontractor, decided to administer some tests designed to gauge our potential. When I was summoned to learn my predicted fate in life, I was told that I "probably would get to go to college" but I "should not count on being able to go to graduate or professional school." I was stunned and shaken by the prognosis, especially as I had been humming along in school, ranked about 10th in a class of about 400 students.

When I got home that evening, I immediately told my parents what had happened. Fortunately, they were reassuring, telling me to pay the test results and the tester no heed whatsoever and to continue on course in school. Thanks to my folks and to a homeroom teacher who was squarely in my corner, this incident of devaluation did not derail me academically. Neither my zest for school nor my grades suffered, and I proceeded from high school to graduate from a great college and an equally great law school.

Teachers who genuinely believe in their students' potential are a potent and positive force in youngsters' lives. Cedric Jennings, the Ballou student who was the subject of Suskind's (1994) riveting article in the *Wall Street Journal*, was spurred on by Clarence Taylor, his chemistry teacher and mentor. Taylor made Cedric's education a personal mission, helping him circumnavigate and survive the perils of achieving in the face of hostility and threats from some classmates who disparaged doing well in school. Taylor urged Cedric to ignore the taunts: "I tell him he's in a long, harrowing race, a marathon, and he can't listen to what's being yelled at him from the sidelines. I tell him those people on the sideline are already out of the race" (para. 47).

Not every child is blessed with savvy and supportive parents and teachers who can help them navigate misdiagnoses or momentary setbacks, not to mention specious or malevolent advice from adults who may not have children's best interests at heart. Adults who rear and educate children need to be attuned to the signals and slights that intentionally or inadvertently devalue youngsters. And they—along with communities—need to create structures and experiences that transmit signals to children that they are indeed highly valued.

For young people, the realization that they are not valued can be dispiriting, just as the reality that they *are* valued can be a revelation. The gradual transformation of Lavin Curry, a troubled and troublesome student at the Chicago Military Academy, demonstrates the difference that valuing a youngster can make. Lavin's commandant and instructors were determined to pull him back from the abyss of academic failure:

> When Lavin Curry arrived at the Chicago Military Academy as a freshman in 1999, he was brash. He was wild. As Frank C. Bacon, the academy's superintendent and a retired Army brigadier general, said of Lavin, "He was a bad little sucker, always into something, always thought he was right."
>
> Lavin couldn't live with his mother and he never met his father. He was raised by his cousin. By the time he got to high school, he was drinking, smoking and ignoring everyone. "I just didn't care about the rules of the school," Lavin recalls. "I didn't think about the consequences of my actions."

One day he got drunk before the first period and passed out in the school bathroom. He was almost kicked out of school. Instead, his instructors and the commandant prodded him to change his behavior and salvage his academic career. Lavin was allowed to stay after he promised to attend a weekend counseling program.

Lavin came to realize that his teachers had simply been trying to give him what he needed: some order in his life. The marching, the saluting, the obeying of rules were all part of turning him into someone who deserved respect.

As Lavin acknowledges, "They changed my life. They fought for me to stay in school. They really cared about me."

Now at 17, he has stopped drinking and smoking. He has bumped his grades up to A's and B's and begun talking about college, maybe even law school. He's also a running back on the football team, sketches Japanese animation characters, and holds a part-time job. (Katz, 2002, p. 1)

Children relish being valued, and they quickly pick up the negative vibes when they aren't. Of course, parents and teachers should value youngsters. But here, too, that is not their job alone. Just as communities go to great lengths to shower tributes on athletes, civic leaders, corporate heads, and other luminaries, so should communities also show young people that they genuinely are valued because, as Urban Leaguers are fond of saying, "Our Children = Our Destiny."

Give Students the Benefits of Belonging

Theories abound about why teenagers belong to street gangs. Researchers cite a wide array of reasons, among them low self-esteem, hunger for respect, limited economic opportunity, peer pressure, physical protection, alienation from parents, financial incentives, communal honor and loyalty, and fellowship (Parker, 2001).

Easily the most memorable and insightful explanation I have ever heard was offered by Tee Rogers, a Los Angeles gang leader, who would know. According to Rogers, "What I think is formulating here is that human nature wants to be accepted. A human being gives less of a damn what he is accepted into. At that age—11 to 17—all kids want to belong. They are unpeople" (Bing, 1989, p. 51).

Although teen gangs are the antithesis of social acceptability, the gangs satisfy a hunger among their members for honor, loyalty, and fellowship, particularly among low-income Latino, black, and white youngsters (Parker, 2001). Some scholars see gangs as any group of youngsters who (1) are generally perceived as a distinct aggregation by others in their neighborhood; (2) recognize themselves as a denotable group, almost invariably with a group name; and (3) have been involved in enough delinquent incidents to call forth a consistent negative response from neighborhood residents and enforcement agencies (Parker, 2001). Gangs typically mark their distinctiveness in visual and audible ways, such as attire, lingo, hand signals, and tattoos.

Violent gang members cite honor as an essential value. They invoke such language as *respect, reputation, self-respect,* and *status* as emblematic of honor, while to them dishonor is tantamount to insult and disrespect. Youth gangs convey honor via initiation rites, collective or communal honor, the inheritance of a good name in association with the collective, and the promise of recognition and a reputation (Parker, 2001).

Although the evidence is often self-reported, research suggests that belonging to positive youth groups may boost participants' self-confidence and curb risky behaviors. As Rosenberg (1999) observes, outcasts need to feel that they belong to a socially acceptable group.

Research and common sense tell us that many problems in schools derive from the desire of young people to belong to a group—a group where they matter, where they are depended on, where their presence or absence is noticed: "Such success (with fringe students) begins by giving students a reason to behave appropriately—by giving them, first, the experience of belonging and contributing to a positive peer group dedicated to a mutually agreed-upon project and, second, the experience of both positive and negative consequences of the peer group's actions" (p. 27).

Other researchers have come to the same conclusion. For example, Goodenow (1993) notes, "Although expectancy of success was the primary predictor of academic effort and grades, the subjective sense of belonging and support was also significantly associated with these outcomes" (p. 37).

Given their sheer size and anonymity, large schools obviously struggle when it comes to fostering an atmosphere of belonging. Smaller schools typically feel and function differently in this respect. Schools and other youth programs that follow a military model do very well at instilling a sense of belonging. Former Boy Scouts, for instance, say that the experience taught them to give their best effort in everything they do and has helped them reject pressure from peers who are up to no good (Harris Interactive, 2005). And youth corps, which can take various forms, attempt to inculcate values that resemble those of both military organizations and social organizations. Like the military, notes CSIS, youth corps also foster internal communities that unite corps members and staff, and thereby create bonds of interdependence and mutual respect. These groups offer settings where young people can develop a sense of belonging and learn individual and collective responsibility (Cullinan et al., 1992). When you add it all up, belonging to a positive peer group provides a reputable vehicle that enables young people to develop constructive values, demonstrate their competence and mastery, and gain recognition for their accomplishments.

Provide Recognition and Rituals

In K–12 education, schools typically recognize and reward the top achievers in any given category, whether for academic accomplishment or community service. This tradition is perfectly understandable. The trouble is that students who are struggling academically or disenchanted with school may perceive these traditional forms of recognition as utterly out of reach. Recognizing this, some schools opt to celebrate a broader array of accomplishments. As one Florida principal whose school follows this practice put it, "I believe that all students need to be motivated, and when you only recognize the 'A' students, you have lost a group of students who think they can never be recognized. . . . We have students set individual goals for reading, math, and writing. When they meet their goals, they are rewarded for their work" ("Honoring Student Achievement," 2004, p. 27).

A principal from California views broadening the definition of what deserves recognition as "a way to reward individual students for reaching their potential, not surpassing others." As another example, Saratoga Middle School in Wyoming has an "Up" and "Down" list that covers academics and behavior. According to Scott Schiller, the principal, "A student could be on one list for academics and another for behavior. The 'Down' list is given to teachers, and parents are notified; the 'Up' list is posted in the school" ("Honoring Student Achievement," 2004, p. 27).

Other organizations and enterprises are even more adept—and flexible—about motivating the broad swath of their charges by demonstrating that their contributions and accomplishments are worthwhile. For example, recognition and rewards are a time-honored way that traditional youth clubs like 4-H, the Boy Scouts, and the Girl Scouts validate members' accomplishments. The 4-H Web site (www.4-h.org) indicates that "4-Hers can compete with their projects in contests at the local, state, regional, or national levels." In the Boy Scouts, youngsters strive to win merit badges and qualify as Eagle Scouts and members of the elite Order of the Arrow.

Ceremonies and rites of passage transmit the critically important message that the accomplishments being recognized, be they imposing or modest, are valued. They also are instrumental in the process of maturation. Society tends to take these rituals for granted. We stage them habitually yet seldom pause to assess why we do so and how they might contribute more powerfully to turning youngsters on to achievement.

General Colin Powell once told me that rites of passage matter enormously in the military where, for instance, it's a big deal for recruits to graduate from basic training, earn the right to be called Marines, and wear the Marine uniform. According to CSIS (2000), "All the services . . . use boot camp or basic training as a rite of passage for new initiates—a critical cog in the turning of civilians into service members—and have adopted hierarchical, youth-oriented, up-or-out systems that allow for few lateral entry opportunities" (p. xviii).

In many religions and cultures, culturally prescribed rites mark "the passage of a person from one social status to another" (Venable, 1997, p. 8). Or as Paul Hill Jr., president of the East End Neighborhood House in Cleveland, puts it, "Rites of passage are those structures, rituals, and ceremonies by which age-class members or individuals in a group successfully come to know who they are and what they are about—the purpose and meaning for their existence, as they proceed from one clearly defined state of existence to the next state or passage in their lives" (Venable, 1997, p. 8). In a more philo-sophical vein, Peter Matthiessen once wrote in the poignant picture album entitled *Circle of Life*, "Rites momentarily lift us from the petty confusions of existence and make us pay complete attention to the passage of our lives, complete attention to the human transformations that link and bind us to all other humans . . . complete attention to the wonder of it all" (cited in Venable, 1997, p. 8).

Rites of passage play a critical socialization role in many reli-gions and cultures. As Venable (1997) describes it, Buddhist children are transformed into adult Buddhists by following the Buddha's own transition from wealth to enlightenment during the Sin Byu cere-mony. At the Jewish bar or bat mitzvah, a 13-year-old child is recog-nized as "son or daughter of the commandment," which means that child is presumed old enough to be responsible for living not only "a Jewish life, but also to sanctify life" (p. 8). Through the kisungu rite, Basange girls in Zaire are initiated into the world of adulthood through the symbolic death of their childhood. Baptism, as a symbol of death to sin and new life in Jesus Christ, serves as a focal rite of passage into full participation within the Christian community. Some experts characterize these as culturally prescribed rites that "accom-pany the passage of a person from one social status to another" (p. 8). Others observe more expansively that rites of passage and the entire ritual process achieve a shift in consciousness appropriate with new social markers or standing.

Most Americans, however, experience no traditional or stan-dardized rite of passage from childhood to adulthood. Instead, "a protracted and amorphous state of adolescence prevails in which bio-logical and psychological transitions are taking place . . . unassisted by ritual processes that would make the transition clear and definite for all involved" (Venable, 1997, p. 8). As Zahniser has written, just when teens need adults the most—namely, in the years of their developing sexuality and cognitive decision-making abilities—our society most clearly leaves them to themselves (cited in Venable, 1997). Rites of passage help adolescents form a new identity and foster a sense of belonging. They bond to the community in a new way, and as a result, they bond to the beliefs and values of that community as well.

As the rite of passage approaches, young people anxiously look forward to "their day." In the process, older members of the community can celebrate and recognize the new adult status of the former child. The progression from childhood to adulthood also means a movement away from parents. In rites of passage, parents almost always participate as spectators, not as key players. Sponsors or mentors, or sometimes unknown adult members of the surrounding tribes, perform the actual rites of initiation and passage in certain cultures. On the topic of rites of passage, Elkind says this:

> We all have a "sense of becoming," of growing and changing as individuals. Markers confirm us in our sense of growing and changing. This confirmation, moreover, has to be social as well as personal. However personally gratifying the attainment of certain markers is, such attainments mean much more when accompanied by social recognition. Indeed, much of the gratification of reaching new markers is the public approval that comes with it. (cited in Venable, 1997, p. 10)

Although rites of passage may be specific to cultures and faiths, it's the ritualistic nature of the experience that is most important rather than the specific steps in the ritual. Many of these rites can be adapted and used by a community for the benefit of all who are willing to accept the challenge for transformation and change. Where adolescents and adults share a common context, appropriate rites can be fashioned for an almost limitless number of educational, social, or religious purposes. Encapsulating the research and real-world experience, Venable (1997) offers this practical advice for recognizing adolescents via rites of passage:

- Target teens nearing the onset of sexual maturity. This may mean including males who are older than participating females;
- Involve parents peripherally, not as principal players;
- Involve as many people from the adolescents' community (family, adults, friends, school, etc.) as possible in rituals of separation and re-incorporation, as well as instructors and mentors during the rites of transition;
- Educate the adolescents' community as to how their operational expectations of the new initiates should change; and
- Celebrate, celebrate, celebrate. (p. 10)

The remainder of this book brings to life this thought-provoking research about the powerful link between student motivation and academic achievement. As you will read, real schools and real educators have forged effective partnerships with real community groups to spur real children to achieve and then salute them publicly when they do. I hope that these heartwarming examples and innovative ideas will inspire school boards, administrators, principals, and teachers to tailor mobilization strategies to their own communities that will inspire their students to strive for academic proficiency and success.

The Essential Information on Student Motivation

- Motivation influences achievement.
- Perceived discrimination and devaluation can dampen motivation.
- Lack of motivation is reversible.
- Motivation can be cultivated and inculcated.
- The military is masterful at motivation.
- Frequent recognition stokes motivation.

3

CELEBRATING STUDENT ACHIEVEMENT

Mobilizing the community usually isn't covered in educators' preservice training or professional development, much less made part of their job description. No wonder it may strike many as a daunting, unfamiliar task. The efforts of National Urban League affiliates—typically in close collaboration with school boards, superintendents, principals, and teachers—to mobilize their communities can provide tangible insights for educators who aspire to enlist their own communities in the cause of helping students succeed. The activities described in this chapter and the next offer concrete ideas, inspiration, and "lessons learned" for educators who see the value of enlisting community groups to help encourage youngsters to learn and achieve.

Launching the Campaign

When I became president of the National Urban League in 1994, many national and local leaders of our movement were as profoundly troubled as I was by the disturbing statistics about the underachievement and nagging achievement gaps that were holding our youngsters back. We were also distressed by anti-intellectualism among some black students, who resisted doing well academically because they claimed it was tantamount to "acting white."

These attitudes and realities bestirred us to mount the Campaign for African-American Achievement. In essence, our goal was to spread the gospel of achievement; more specifically, we set out to galvanize children, families, and communities to care about academic achievement and literacy. I readily confess that back then I wasn't steeped in the kind of research cited in this book. My colleagues and I were basically running on instinct, outrage, and anxiety about the future of our children and our people.

The traditional response of social service agencies to a problem like poorly educated children and children slacking off in school is to mount direct service programs that provide assistance to a finite group of youngsters. We didn't go that route because we were convinced that the scale of the underachievement phenomenon far outstripped our capacity to serve all of the young people directly. What's more, I doubted that there was enough government and philanthropic money to do the job. And, frankly, I felt that families and communities had to step up and take responsibility for boosting student commitment to achievement rather than look to outsiders to do that job for them. If an academic culture is truly to take hold and endure, it must be embedded in the hearts and minds—and the belief systems and behaviors—of youngsters, their families, and the organizations that make up their communities.

Therefore, the National Urban League opted for a *community mobilization* strategy. More specifically, we concentrated on engaging those major organizations that composed the enduring social infrastructure of the black community: black churches, sororities, fraternities, civic clubs, and professional associations.

Two summits produced consensus on the basic elements of the Achievement Campaign, which the participating organizations then asked the Urban League to spearhead, nationally and locally, and which they pledged to embrace. The three basic strategies of the campaign were as follows:

1. Spread the gospel that "Achievement Matters," so that parents, students, and community leaders fully understand the imperative that our children achieve at high levels.

2. Transform parents into sophisticated consumers of public education so that they properly support the academic and social development of their youngsters at home, in the community, and in school.

3. Create a consumer demand for quality education, so that educators and policymakers fulfill their obligations to our children.

National vision and initiatives are fine. But the heart of the Achievement Campaign was what happened in communities where young people are reared, nurtured, and educated. More to the point of this book, this is where the communities that must be mobilized also live. Some 45 Urban League affiliates signed on as "Pacesetter Affiliates," agreeing to implement the three strategies locally.

The rest of this chapter describes the primary ways that we set about mobilizing communities to help boost student achievement. In my estimation, we accomplished much, oftentimes beyond our expectations. I witnessed, up close and personal, what's possible when schools and community groups take mobilization seriously and make sure the organizing gears mesh.

Although I retired as president of the National Urban League in 2003, the Achievement Campaign inspires me still. There is no surefire guide for mobilizing communities, but firsthand experience shows beyond doubt that it can be done by educators (and other villagers) who are determined to motivate the children in their community to achieve in school and succeed in life.

Achievement Month

The dawn of the new school year energizes schoolchildren as well as their parents and teachers. It generates excitement and anticipation, providing a perfect occasion to set goals, expectations, and benchmarks for the year to come.

The resumption of school provides, therefore, the perfect occasion for the community to demonstrate that it values academic achievement, that it is deeply invested in its children's education, and that it intends to do its part to help the schools and schoolchildren succeed. In other words, members of the community could and should use the launch of the new school year to signal to parents, children, and educators alike that they are "going back to school" too.

In this spirit, the National Urban League and its affiliates kicked off the 1996–1997 school year by designating September 1996 as "Achievement Month." On the third Saturday of September, all across the United States, our affiliates and their community partners staged block parties, street festivals, assemblies, and parades to herald the new school year and encourage schoolchildren to learn and achieve in the year ahead. Holding all these events on the same day demonstrated the power and potential of organizing communities around the common theme of achievement. Across the country that day, as many as 50,000 youngsters and parents participated in Achievement Month activities.

Although we celebrated Achievement Month on the same day, the affiliates didn't use a cookie-cutter approach to doing so. For instance, in Gary, Indiana, the Urban League of Northwest Indiana and its Achievement Campaign partners staged a back-to-school parade for 10,000 students. The Pittsburgh Urban League held a "Shout About Youth" celebratory boat ride for 400 youngsters. In Louisville, the local campaign mounted a Youth Appreciation Day involving 700 children.

Gena Davis Watkins, former senior vice president and chief development officer for the National Urban League, vividly recalls the Achievement Month rallies that she attended (personal communication, February 2, 2007). In Atlanta, she remembers, the Achievement Month rally was held at Martin Luther King High School. Nine hundred excited students and parents filled the auditorium. Each youngster received an Achievement Matters statuette with his or her name on it. A local rap group, the Goodie Mob, performed for the hometown crowd. At one point, they stopped the show to talk with the students about the importance of staying in school and getting a diploma—something they lamented that they hadn't done. The students paid rapt attention to the rappers' message.

In Champaign, Illinois, the local Urban League staged a two-day Achievement Matters Fair patterned after a county fair. Featured attractions ran the gamut from rides on Ferris wheels to a book-reading contest. The youngsters conducted technology and poetry presentations. An estimated 2,500 people came to the fair.

The Urban League in Cincinnati turned its Achievement Month event into a full-blown Education Summit, opening the city's convention center to students, parents, and members of community groups. A Parent Empowerment Forum kicked off the summit, and it was followed the next day by parent workshops and workshops for 7th through 12th graders on topics such as overcoming barriers, preventing students from dropping out, and stemming violence. The summit made the hoped-for impression on 13-year-old Harun Shabazz, who said, "You won't make it in life without an education. And I'm going to be successful" (Hayes, 2001).

Plenty of youngsters like Harun heard our message that academic achievement matters and is something to work for and be proud of. It obviously helped that our messengers—from Tom Joyner and Magic Johnson to the Goodie Mob and other local celebrities— were cool in the eyes of the kids. In fact, one of the youngsters actually asked me what had taken adults so long to find them and support them. Another agitated young fellow accosted me after one rally, explaining how well he was doing in school. He was visibly upset that he hadn't been recognized at the rally. I apologized profusely that we had missed him and urged him not to let up academically.

We Love a Parade

If you really want to generate excitement about something, consider holding a parade. Just think about the festive mood, the pageantry, and the basic message of all those parades over the years that pay tribute to returning war veterans, sports champions, gay pride, or ethnic pride.

The Urban League in Gary, Indiana, has experience with parades. For many years it staged an annual back-to-school rally called the "Parade 4 Education" (Puente, 1997). The parade covered a mile-long route that ran along Gary's 5th Avenue, culminated in an educational fair and performances, and routinely drew more than 5,000 students from every city public school. The student participants were accompanied by floats and marching bands. Sponsors have included the Gary Accord, Gary Community School Corps, City of Gary, and the Council of PTAs.

One year, the parade highlighted the accomplishments of the fabled Tuskegee Airmen and showcased aviation careers. Quentin P. Smith, a former Tuskegee Airman as well as a school administrator and principal, served as honorary grand marshal (Paul, 1998). Spicing up the parades were clowns and tumblers and even Miss USA delegates. And some years, the parade culminated with the Gary Air Show in Marquette Park, where youngsters between the ages of 7 and 17 got free airplane rides. The parade has also had distinct, academic themes. One year, "Reading: Key to Success" was the watchword. That parade drew roughly 6,500 marchers and 8,000 onlookers. Every child who marched received free books and a book bag (DeNeal, 2000).

Inspired by these examples, I can readily imagine educators collaborating with community groups to stage annual Achievement Day parades through the heart of town to celebrate the accomplishments of students who, I would suggest, pass the obligatory state exams in reading and math. Pegging the threshold for marching at such a modest level may offend purists. But given the sheer scale of underachievement, we need to cast the net of encouragement and recognition as widely as is legitimately possible.

Skeptics may question the worth of rituals like parades or even dismiss them as one-shot events unlikely to make a lasting difference. Quite the contrary. Communities cling steadfastly to parades and ceremonies because they are powerful vehicles for celebrating accomplishments and transmitting cherished values from one generation to the next. Parades are time-honored spectacles that lure sizable and enthusiastic audiences, attract media attention, and transmit messages. That's undoubtedly why parades featuring schoolchildren strike such a positive chord with kids and adults. The mother of one marcher in Gary observed, "One of the biggest things we always looked forward to was the parade. You were important because you were in the parade. . . . Kids need something to look forward to" (DeNeal, 2000). Adis Foley, a high school junior who marched in Gary, echoed this sentiment by noting that the parade there boosts pride in their schools, their city, and themselves: "I'm not here because I had to. I wanted to be here because I am proud of my school and the city. We have good students of all ages who are supported by our parents and our teachers. We care about our education" (DeNeal, 1997).

A parade is an ideal vehicle for educators to forge high-profile collaborations whose sole purpose is to signal loudly and clearly to young people that academic achievers are the community's heroes. To pull off these parades, educators could form coalitions of local groups like the Urban League and NAACP affiliates; sororities, fraternities, and civic groups; schools and libraries; local education funds; business associations like Chamber of Commerce; local offices of large corporations; and community and family foundations, United Ways, and public officials. Another potential partner—indeed, an indispensable one—is the nearest expert who actually knows how to stage parades.

Achievement Fairs

When I was a child, my parents sometimes took my brother and me to Pennsylvania's sprawling York County Fair. I always got a kick out of the tacky games and Ferris wheels, as well as the aroma of fried dough and the competitions for best-in-class cows, sheep, bunnies, chicks, and guinea pigs raised by members of the local 4-H clubs. What I never appreciated until researching this book was the role that fairs like these can play in motivating youngsters to achieve and then display their accomplishments to approving adults.

As Porter (1997) writes of Wisconsin's Bauer County Fair, its enduring attraction is that its central mission, unchanged over the years, is public education: "[The fair] has provided a uniquely effective, non-school means through which traditional cultural values, skills, and relationships are transmitted from generation to generation. Through the intergenerational events that constitute the fair, young participants are drawn into an engaging community celebration of both learning and belonging" (p. 179). Through the fair, youth clubs such as Future Farmers of America (FFA) and Future Homemakers of America (FHA), the Boy and Girl Scouts, and 4-H provide organized means for young people to develop skills and then bring exhibits to the fair. Furthermore, the county fair nicely complements the formal education received in school. Porter continues: "The fair provides a unique public forum for celebrating achievement and inspiring excellence. It is a time to focus on the positive. It may be seen as a complement to the schools, strategically providing educational elements that are not highlighted in the standardized curriculum" (p. 191).

The experience makes a decided impression on the young participants. The children who do projects for the Bauer County Fair may be chided by their nonfarming peers in school as "hicks." But the fair serves as a safe space where farm youth are among those given center stage. As one student explained, her interest in the kinds of activities recognized at the fair was allowed free and unabashed expression there: "In school, they'd make fun of you. They don't know me as anything but a 'sports jock.' But at the fair, these interests are validated" (Porter, 1997, p. 193).

My elementary school in Washington, D.C., staged a small-scale version of a county fair, only it focused exclusively on science projects. For our annual science fair, every student in the school prepared a science project that was then displayed in the lunchroom. Probably the most popular experiment among the kids was suspending a tooth in a glass of soda pop and then monitoring how long the tooth took to disintegrate entirely due to the sugar. Whatever it was we budding scientists created, family members would visit the science fair and listen proudly and patiently as we chattered away about our projects.

Imagine, then, an annual achievement fair that is staged in a large indoor venue like a convention center or local armory. Alternatively, it could be held outdoors, provided plenty of tents are used. If physical space or organizational capacity is a consideration, this annual fair could be open to a specific portion of the student population—say, to all 7th graders—an approach that would ensure virtually all students will get to participate during the course of their school careers. If space permits, there could be fairs for two or more grade levels each year.

What exactly would an achievement fair spotlight? I envision students being invited to prepare a display on an academically related topic of their choosing, as opposed to an assignment meted out by their teachers. Some youngsters might do science projects. Others might engineer and build small structures. Still other students might want to present mini-research projects, skits, poems, and short stories. The presentations of the student projects could run the gamut from displays to recitations and performances. The skills they use to prepare their projects would have to mirror those cultivated in school, like reading, writing, research, calculation, and so forth. As with the science fairs of my youth, schools could strongly encourage every student to participate, perhaps even offering extra academic credit to those who do.

The achievement fair could, in fact, be a two-step affair. The first phase would be held in schools or community centers, where the students' projects are judged on several levels—first place, second, third, and honorable mention. Those awarded one of these prizes would qualify to display their wares at the citywide or community-wide achievement fair. What's more, every child who prepared a presentation would receive a certificate or some other form of recognition.

Needless to say, it's critically important for the children's parents, family members, and friends to turn out. The fairs could be held over the weekend so the adults have several shots at showing up. Given the customary pride that parents have in their youngsters' accomplishments, this should not be a problem. In the final analysis, the key is for the youngsters to undertake projects that genuinely interest them and for the community writ large to salute them for their effort and talent.

Recognition Events

A time-honored method of motivating students is via recognition luncheons and receptions, typically held toward the end of the school year. One annual event of this kind occurs in Westchester County, New York, where I live. The Black Scholars Recognition Reception, which is held these days at Manhattanville College, began in 1985. It started out as a luncheon but evolved into a reception when the planners decided to devote the money raised to student awards instead of to full-course meals.

Ernest Prince, the CEO of the Westchester Urban League, got the ball rolling when he invited the heads of a number of black civic and social groups to explore what they could do together to improve conditions for black people in the county. The leaders discussed various needs, including employment, before zeroing in on education as their collective focus. In particular, they expressed concern that schoolchildren who were doing well in school weren't getting the recognition they deserved. Top scholars and athletes got recognition, but the groups felt that wasn't good enough. In their view, there was no focus on identifying students who were doing well academically, if not at the top of the charts, and the community didn't recognize them. Also, they worried that there was no public acknowledgment of the solid job done by the parents and caregivers of these achievers. Finally, they felt a need to send a strong, clear, and consistent message to the school systems in Westchester County that many people in the black community cared about academic achievement.

The Black Scholars Recognition event crystallized as the way these groups intended to send this message to children, parents, and schools. A cross section of black social and civic organizations signed on to help plan and stage the event. These days, the steering committee consists of representatives of approximately 20 community organizations, social and professional groups, corporations, and churches.

At the ceremony, the students receive plaques as well as proclamations from the Westchester County executive. What's more, some of them receive monetary prizes. In 2006, for instance, seven students received $1,000 scholarships, and five others got gifts of $250 for books. To deal with the fact that all of the students actually qualify for these awards, the winners' names are chosen from a drum on the morning of the ceremony. In conjunction with the recognition event, the planning committee also started an essay contest, which is funded by PepsiCo and awards five prizes ranging from $300 to $1,000.

The number of high school graduates recognized has grown steadily over the years, from about 150 graduates at the first luncheon more than 20 years ago to roughly 300 in recent years. The ceremony has generated media coverage over the years, including, in 2007, a significant front-page story in the main regional newspaper. Sometimes the local newspapers print the youngsters' essays or excerpts from them. The newspapers occasionally print the names of all of the scholars.

Educators in Westchester County see the merits of this celebration. As one high school guidance counselor wrote to Ernest Prince, "As far back as I can remember in my career as a school counselor and director of guidance over a span of more than three decades, and as long as this initiative has been in progress, I have been proud to send you the names of our Black Scholar candidates. Over that same time, I have never missed a June convocation of these wonderful students (personal communication, Winter 2006)." Planning for the event begins by considering the fact that the county contains some 34 public and private high schools. Each year the organizers reach out to the school systems and the high schools to get them to agree to identify black seniors who are at or above the 3.0 GPA threshold that is required to qualify for recognition. This means they must have maintained a *B* average throughout their high school career, not just in a few marking periods.

In the beginning, some school districts and individual schools leapt at the opportunity for their youngsters to be recognized and provided the names and addresses of eligible students. Others, however, were reluctant to supply the information on the grounds that they'd be identifying only black students, not all *B* students of every race. They felt this was a violation of student privacy. Many members of the planning group in Westchester are active or retired educators. To overcome this resistance, they visited officials in their school systems to try to persuade them to participate. They negotiated compromises that asked schools, for instance, to provide the Urban League with the names and addresses of *B* students so that the Urban League itself could contact them and invite them to the recognition event. Other schools insisted that the Urban League send the information about the event to the school, which would then pass it on to the qualified students and their parents. The planning committee has made do with whatever arrangements get the word out, one way or the other, to students and their parents.

In Westchester, the funds that are raised to stage the ceremony and provide the awards by and large come from the participating organizations themselves. Some of the funding comes from corporations like PepsiCo. But, as Prince insists, the key to the community "owning" and sustaining the recognition ceremony for 21 years has been the fact that the bulk of the money comes from community groups themselves. In fact, the sponsoring groups commit up front to cover all of the costs of the event and awards. Donations from individuals and groups range from $25 to $1,000. Every community organization that is aligned with the effort contributes. Even though many of them have their own scholarship programs, their commitment to this effort is on top of that. As recently as 2005, the planning committee raised $20,500. The recognition event itself cost $8,200. The remainder went for the awards.

According to Prince, there has never been a problem keeping the volunteer groups involved over the years. Once they attend the recognition event and see the enthusiasm and impact firsthand, they are hooked. The room is bursting with energy. The scholars assemble and march in school by school. Parents watch proudly as their young scholars are called up individually to receive their plaques and proclamations.

Other communities have staged ceremonies akin to the one in Westchester County. Local groups in Tacoma, Washington, for example, launched such an effort in the mid-1990s. It was sponsored by the Partner Community Organizations, a coalition of six predominantly black community organizations ("Students Get Push," 1997). The event, known as the Elizabeth Wesley Youth Merit Incentive Award

Program Luncheon, was held annually at the Allen African Methodist Episcopal Church.

To win an award, students must have earned a 2.5 GPA, have 90 percent attendance, secure three recommendations, and write an essay covering the topics of academic achievement, community involvement, and good citizenship. In the first year of the event, only five students qualified (or at least came forward). By the second year, 45 winners received awards of $350 each. Their pictures were then displayed at the Tacoma Mall throughout the summer.

To stage the event and pay for the awards, the coalition in Tacoma tapped a wide array of sources. It raised $16,000 from nearly 60 individuals, most of whom were members of the black community. The giant retailer Nordstrom pitched in with a contribution of $1,500.

The Urban League in Broward County, Florida, has conducted a Salute to Scholars event for roughly a decade. It is held at the Broward Performing Arts Center. Some two dozen organizations participate. As Don Bowen, the former CEO of the affiliate, explained to me, each of these groups first gives out college scholarships at its own events, and then they join forces to present these awards a second time at this event. This way, every group retains its organizational profile while coalescing to make an even bigger deal out of academic achievement than each could on its own.

Recognition events like these are straightforward affairs, hardly exotic or highly innovative. Yet they make a decided impression on the students and their parents. As the chair of the Westchester event, retired corporate executive Dorothy Orr, once said, "Many of these students were intellectually harassed. They're called nerd or Oreo" (Eisenberg, 1996, p. 8). That is why it is so heartening to hear stories of these scholars taking their plaques to college and mounting them on the walls of their dorm rooms.

A 2007 article in the *Washington Post* reports that the District of Columbia College Success Foundation staged a high-energy ceremony at the Town Hall Education Arts and Recreation campus to pay tribute to 201 high school seniors selected for the DC Achievers program. During their final year in high school, these academically promising students will participate in precollege seminars and get help with applying to college. According to the article (Labbé, 2007), the students' sense of accomplishment about having been selected was palpable. As 17-year-old Kevin Jones of Maya Angelou Public Charter School remarked excitedly, "I wasn't thinking about college before. It's like a door opened and this is the first step to success. Now it's up to me" (p. 8).

Rewarding Good Behavior

Mind you, the National Urban League's Achievement Campaign wasn't solely about promoting academic achievement. It also aimed to encourage young people to behave themselves and serve their communities. After all, satisfying and productive lives grow out of a combination of these ingredients, not from any one to the exclusion of the others. That is why our affiliates staged events during the school year to celebrate young people who, to invoke the title of Spike Lee's 1989 film, "Do the Right Thing." These events enabled us to pay tribute to young people for accomplishments and contributions to their communities that often go unheralded.

The basic idea behind these events was for community members to signal, loudly and clearly, what kinds of behavior they value. In sharp contrast to the incessant media coverage of black youngsters committing murder and mayhem, the Urban League affiliates sought to use these celebratory events to garner more favorable coverage of youngsters who are striving to help themselves and others. These events sometimes were the featured event during Achievement Month. But they often were held at other times of the school year. Elizabeth Nicholson, a retired schoolteacher who coordinated these events in Lorain County, Ohio, summarized the essence of the idea when she said, "We want to celebrate those young children who have done positive things to make our community richer and better. There are students from all over the county who are known to have shown improvement in their studies this year" (Brown, 1996).

In 1996, the first year of the Achievement Campaign, 90 Urban League affiliates organized block parties, parades, fairs, public rallies, award luncheons, and recognition dinners to honor students for "doing the right thing." The inaugural celebration took place on April 30 at my alma mater, Coolidge High School in Washington, D.C. (Kyriakos, 1996). After a lineup of preachy adult speakers (including myself) who undoubtedly tested the teenagers' patience, we turned to honoring a number of them for their scholastic accomplishments and community service. Maudine R. Cooper, CEO of the host Urban League, captured the essence of the ceremony when she observed, "This is not an elitist program. You can't always be number one in academics. But somewhere in your life, you can be number one in something, and that is what we're celebrating" (Kyriakos, 1996, p. D3).

In Hudson County, New Jersey, the Urban League used the Doing the Right Thing event to bestow some positive attention on adolescents for a change—after all the local news coverage of youth gangs, muggings, and other crime. The Youth Celebration Day was held at Jersey City's Lincoln Park. Two hundred students were selected to be honored from among nominees submitted by local schools, churches, community organizations, youth clubs, and community leaders. The youngsters were honored for simple things like doing well in school and volunteering to help their communities in their spare time.

Melissa Escobar, a junior at Holy Family Academy who had helped younger students with their homework at the Greenville Branch Library in Jersey City, appreciated the recognition: "The way society is now, older people judge all teenagers as bad and in trouble. But we're not all like that. A lot of us are intelligent and go to school and have hopes for the future. I concentrate on my school work, and on helping people out" (Petrick, 1997, p. A5).

The recognition events also struck Pat Smith, a guidance counselor at Sulphur Springs Elementary School in Tampa, Florida, as valuable. Noting that several youngsters in her school with behavioral problems had made a change for the better, she remarked that celebrating children who did the right thing helps make a difference: "They need to know that everyone is watching them, and they can make a difference" (Parker, 1997, p. 1).

In addition to the customary celebration of academic achievement and community service, the Portland Urban League added a new wrinkle. Dozens of booths were set up in a field in Portland, devoted to topics such as college admissions and tutoring. Next to the field, the public library staged a book fair where each child who had completed the fair's activities received free books (Daniels, 1997; "March, Book Fair," 1997; "March Set to Promote," 1997). This component featured local leaders, called "People Who Read," who talked to the children about their enjoyment of reading. The book fair attracted the sponsorship of Washington Mutual Bank. Students like Etopi Fanta, a junior at Lincoln High School, clearly got the point of the celebration: "A lot of people think that African Americans are all about negative things. We are trying to show that, like everyone else, we can achieve everything we want to" (Daniels, 1997). Or as Gerald Carroll, a 17-year-old honoree in San Diego, put it, "They see us getting good grades and think, 'I can be cool and carry books at the same time'" (Santana, 2000, p. B2).

The Urban League in Hartford, Connecticut, took its celebration to the highest-profile venue in the state. On September 20, 1997, nearly 1,000 people trekked to the state capitol to celebrate youth who had done the right thing (LeGrier, 1997). The theme that day was to encourage the city's youth to work hard, remain focused, and keep the faith that good things will happen (Rully, 1997). The five-hour rally received widespread support from a broad array of organizations, the media, and state officials. One television station broadcast news updates throughout the morning. The Hartford Public Library docked a bookmobile nearby. Cartoonist Joe Young unrolled sections of his "World's Longest Comic Strip" on the lawn of the state capitol. Other attractions included rollerboarding urban Boy Scouts, the Weaver High School Junior ROTC cadets, and the Unique Drillers. State Sen. Eric Coleman captured the spirit of the rally when he observed, "This is a reaffirmation that we have positive, talented, and productive young people in this community" (Rully, 1997, p. 13).

In San Diego, the Urban League staged the initial Doing the Right Thing rallies during September in conjunction with back-to-school activities. Jimma McWilson, director of the Achievement Campaign for the affiliate, recalls sending letters to the churches explaining the Achievement Campaign and offering to mount a Doing the Right Thing event in each church (personal communication, December 2006). He sought to capitalize on the fact that churches have their own built-in mechanism for organizing and conducting events right at the church. Typically the pastor would invite a guest speaker to make a presentation to young people and their families. This presentation would be followed by a reception after the service, where a *Read and Rise* guide (with tips for parents to help kids read) and other materials would be distributed to families. The Urban League generally gave a half-dozen Doing the Right Thing presentations in churches annually.

These highly diverse rallies attracted an equally diverse array of local partners and cosponsors eager to join in celebrating youth who do the right thing. The imposing range of groups ran the gamut from social organizations and civic outfits to government agencies and business groups. For instance, in Winston-Salem, North Carolina, the collaborators included the Forsyth County Public Health Department, North Carolina Black Repertory Company, Coca-Cola, the City Recreation Department and Housing Authority, community churches, Winston-Salem State University, the Winston-Salem/Forsyth County Schools, the Library Association, and the *Winston-Salem Chronicle*.

A similar celebration orchestrated by the Urban League in New Orleans attracted the cooperation and support of 14 black civic and service organizations, among them the Alpha Kappa Alpha and Delta Sigma Theta sororities, the Alpha Phi Alpha fraternity, family groups like Jack and Jill, and women's groups like the Crescent City and Ponchartrain chapters of the Links, Incorporated and the 100 Black Women.

Cosponsors of the events in other communities included the Black McDonald's Owners Association, local community colleges, and retail giants like Sears Roebuck and Marshall Field's. Local newspapers often pitched in with extensive and enthusiastic coverage. For instance, the *Chronicle-Telegram* in Lorain County, Ohio, listed all 370 students who were recognized for making a constructive difference in their schools and communities. The lesson from these lists is that community organizations are eager to enlist in efforts to motivate children to achieve and to celebrate them for doing so.

In some cases, the celebrations were preceded by a nomination process, including a 150-word essay submitted by a parent, adult, sibling, or friend that cited a notable contribution by the nominee to the community. The selections for recognition were based on the candidates' academic excellence, community service, and leadership. At some celebrations, youngsters received awards, scholarships, and prizes. The amounts may have been modest, such as $5,000 divvied up among 25 awardees, but the message behind them was affirming.

Evaluating Celebrations

Do rallies and celebrations really make an impression on young people? Admittedly, the Urban League did not conduct a rigorous, state-of-the-art evaluation of the Achievement Campaign. Even so, it was reassuring to see what State Farm learned from a preliminary assessment that it commissioned to gauge the early impact of the achievement rallies and Doing the Right Thing events that it promoted and helped underwrite in collaboration with Urban League affiliates. Without getting carried away, given the nature of the assessment, we were encouraged by the young attendees' reactions. Those surveyed said that

• Their grades and attendance had improved, and they were more prone to be on time to class;

• They were more likely now to use a computer, bring their textbooks home, do their daily homework, and do so with fewer distractions from television or CDs; and

• They were more inclined now to go on to college or other forms of postsecondary education and thus more likely to register for the SAT or ACT college entrance exam.

Survey findings like these are instructive and affirming. Even more inspiring are the reactions to these recognition events by students like Nykeesha Davis, a 17-year-old who was honored for her determination and motivation. As she exclaimed to a newspaper reporter, "I tell them, 'you can do anything you want.' They believe this myth that people who are on public assistance and have a single parent are the scum of D.C., are dumb kids. I live in a bad neighborhood, but I've made all A's all my life" (Kyriakos, 1996, p. D3).

Ways to Celebrate Student Achievement

- Proclaim September as "Achievement Month."
- Stage rallies, assemblies, and street festivals to herald the new school year and convey the message that achievement is cool.
- Hold a citywide Achievement Day parade at the end of the school year.
- Salute every student who passes the mandatory state exams.
- Enlist the media to recognize these achievers as municipal heroes, and give them all keys to the city.

4

PROMOTING ACADEMIC SUCCESS

Ceremonies and celebrations are time-honored and immensely effective ways of motivating students to achieve, but they are just the beginning of what must be an ongoing effort. During the National Urban League's Achievement Campaign, many of the activities and events mounted by our affiliates and by other groups focused directly on continued support for students' demonstrated academic success.

Supporting Literacy

As bona fide educators know far better than I, literacy and achievement go hand in glove. Children who proceed through school reading far below grade level face an uphill climb for the rest of their lives. Those distressing NAEP reading statistics that I cited at the beginning of this book underscore why galvanizing communities to promote literacy is an integral part of motivating youngsters to achieve. Urban League affiliates and other groups have gone about it in some novel ways.

Mass "Readathons"

The Urban League in Gary, Indiana, once staged a mass "readathon," where more than 6,000 schoolchildren gathered in the town's baseball stadium to read in unison. (They read *The Eagles Who Thought They Were Chickens* by Mychal Wynn.) This event even earned a mention in the *Guinness Book of World Records*.

Eloise Gentry, the head of Gary's local Urban League, is masterful at mobilizing needed resources at nominal cost. For this event, she got the school districts in the city and surrounding communities to collaborate, even synchronizing the timing with the schools' normal bus schedules so that the children could be brought to and from the stadium at no extra charge. In effect, the school districts treated the event as a mammoth field trip. After it ended, the buses took the children home, just as they would after school.

Once the students arrived at the stadium, they were escorted in by a band. Promptly at 1:00 p.m., someone hoisted a baton as the signal for the youngsters to read in unison. The youngsters finished reading the book in about 15 minutes. At that point, the stadium lights suddenly came on, and the scoreboard erupted in celebration. This grand stunt made a loud statement to the children about the delights of reading.

Organizing an event of this magnitude took considerable effort and perseverance. The Urban League initially expected 5,000 students to participate. When it became apparent that many more would show up, officials had to scramble at the 11th hour to obtain a couple thousand more books so that every child would receive his or her own copy as promised.

The Urban League in Gary manages to mobilize so many volunteer and in-kind resources because it has a reputation for focusing uncompromisingly on the best interests of children and on the issues of literacy and achievement. Gentry, the CEO, and her main collaborator are both educators who are well known to the school system and who know their way around it. The Urban League is especially adept at getting government agencies and businesses to pitch in at minimal expense. It secured the stadium for free because the City of Gary either owned or influenced its use. With a minuscule staff of two, the CEO routinely leverages her 40-member board by persuading them to donate resources they have that she needs and to use their influential contacts on behalf of the Urban League's initiatives for children. In other words, Gentry identifies who controls the resources that she needs and then sets about persuading those who possess these resources to work with her to make them available to implement her plan. She is determined and will pursue them until they consent to give her what she needs for the children.

Literacy Olympiads

A mass readathon is by no means the only method designed to generate student excitement about reading. The Urban League in Winston-Salem, North Carolina, adopted a different but no less innovative approach to promoting literacy. Beginning in the mid-1990s and continuing until 2005, the Urban League partnered with the public library and a local bookstore to stage an annual Literacy Olympiad for middle school students.

As Dee Wylie, the former CEO of the Winston-Salem Urban League, recalled, the Olympiad commenced each year on Martin Luther King's birthday in January and concluded on the last day of February, the end of Black History Month. Roughly 200 youngsters participated each year (personal communication, November 6, 2006). Guidance counselors in the schools promoted the event and helped recruit youngsters by disseminating notices and encouraging participation. In addition, the Urban League enlisted adult mentors who agreed to team up with middle school pupils. Mentors were recruited from churches and community organizations. They then participated in a mentoring workshop to prep them for the assignment.

Together the students and their mentors visited the library to choose the books that the youngsters would read. They picked books with an African American theme. The main library selected appropriate books from its collection and displayed them in a featured section. A local black bookstore collaborated with the Literacy Olympiad as well.

Youngsters earned points based on the number of books they had completed. The books were weighted according to relative degree of difficulty, with children earning more points for more challenging texts. The students would also recount the stories of the books to their mentors, who agreed to read the selections beforehand so they would be able to assess the accuracy of these summaries.

At the conclusion of each year's Literacy Olympiad, the sponsors held a banquet to recognize all students who participated—from those who read dozens of books to those who read just one. Every participant earned a certificate and a book. Additionally, the three children who accumulated the most points received a monetary prize: $25 to the second runner-up, $50 to the first runner-up, and $100 to the winner.

The closing banquet was typically attended by roughly 300 youngsters, parents, and mentors. Wylie recalled that for many parents, this was the first time their child had ever received recognition for anything, much less for an accomplishment related to academics. The proud parents would stand tall beside their children at the banquet. The event generated quite a buzz about reading, along with media coverage, especially in the black press.

The Olympiad and closing banquet were not costly undertakings. The Urban League secured a modest grant from the state to cover the cost of the books given to the children. The banquet was held at the Urban League headquarters, and a local caterer provided food at a modest cost. Businesses and individuals could sponsor a young participant for $50 to $100. Corporate sponsors included R. J. Reynolds, PepsiCo, local banks, Sara Lee, and other local companies that traditionally supported the Winston-Salem Urban League.

Operationally, the Olympiad was not difficult to organize and implement. In theory, the size of the school population posed the only limitation on the potential number of participants, although care was taken to ensure that it did not swell so large that it could not be managed. A steering committee composed of parents, faith-based groups, representatives of the libraries and school system, and Urban League staff and volunteer guild oversaw the effort throughout the year. Recruiting mentors, especially from the ranks of deacons and trustees in the churches, was seldom a problem.

Although the Literacy Olympiad emphasized books with African American themes and was keyed to relevant dates in the calendar, there is no reason why a school system and community groups could not partner to hold similar events for the broadest array of students, choose different themes, and run them other times of the year.

According to Wylie, the Literacy Olympiad introduced youngsters to African American books and subject matter that they had not been exposed to before. This exposure enriched their understanding of who they were as a people. The feedback from the students, she noted, was that many of them didn't particularly enjoy reading prior to participating in the Olympiad. But that changed. Some students even began to urge their school libraries to carry books related to the black experience.

Fifty Books and a Bike

In the late 1990s, school officials in Mount Vernon, a suburb just north of New York City, trained their sights on literacy. The district's student population was about 78 percent black, 14 percent Latino, and 7 percent white. Fifty-six percent of the students qualified for free or reduced-price lunch (Mount Vernon City School District, 2006).

For years, black children in particular had fared badly in Mount Vernon's public schools. A newly elected school board hired an aggressive superintendent named Ronald Ross, who focused every elementary school on improving children's reading and literacy skills. The superintendent, an impatient activist from the 1960s who is passionate about boosting student achievement, set an urgent tone by warning teachers that they must either believe their pupils can achieve or find other work (Ross, 2001).

The superintendent and his team analyzed the state reading exam to determine what skills were required to pass and exactly where the schools were falling short, classroom by classroom and teacher by teacher. To cite just a few of the measures they took, the district instituted professional development for principals and teachers, bringing them together to share ideas and best practices. Reading specialists visited every 4th grade classroom every day. Every elementary school established a daily "literacy bloc": 90 consecutive minutes of reading silently or aloud. The schools offered after-school tutorials.

When State Superintendent of Schools Richard Mills proclaimed that schoolchildren should read 25 books per year, Superintendent Ross decided, in poker parlance, to call and raise him by doubling the goal. To spur extracurricular reading, Ross challenged the pupils to read at least 50 books in a year and to write book reports about what they had read. Those who met or exceeded the target would receive free bicycles. Parents and teachers had to verify that the children actually had done the reading.

The competition paralleled an effort in the schools to stimulate children to read. Ross instituted nightly take-home reading assignments for all 1st through 4th graders and gave the students free backpacks to tote home their books. The youngsters were required to get an adult to sign off that someone had read with the child for at least 30 minutes the previous evening. Ross recalls the heart-wrenching story of a 2nd grader who lived in the Levister Towers projects in Mount Vernon's south end. The youngster had to run up and down the stairs of his building, knocking on the doors and trying to get some adult to read to him because his mother wasn't at home.

Ross originally figured that the number of winners would be modest enough that if he and members of his cabinet bought several bikes, that would be sufficient. He planned to place the names of all youngsters who hit the target in a drum and select five of them to receive free bicycles. To his surprise, nearly 170 of the students completed at least 50 books. Another 570 read between 40 and 49 books. The top scorer was a black boy in the 5th grade who had read 82 books. The runner-up was another 5th grade black boy who had read 81 books. All totaled, over 1,600 youngsters read 25 or more books that year (Ross, 2001). With many more youngsters qualifying than expected, Ross solicited donations from local businesses and community groups to give all of the "winners" free bikes. Teachers and principals donated bikes. Churches pitched in and donated bikes. In fact, the pastors competed to outdo one another.

The competition kicked off in the fall of 2000 and culminated near the end of the school year. The awards ceremony was held on a Saturday. Winners lined up by school to receive their new bikes, as well as helmets. Police officers were on hand to register the bikes. The local newspaper and cable news channel covered the event. Ross was buoyed by some moving letters that he received from the winners' parents.

One academician expressed concern that the winners received bikes rather than awards that were more directly related to literacy.

This placed a higher value on bicycles than on reading, according to the critic. Ross's retort was that students respond to incentives and that the prospect of winning new bikes could motivate them to read. He continued: "All of us want positive reinforcement. These kids are going to be reading long after they stop riding a bike. And guess what—these kids will have read 50 more books than they would have read" (Wilson, 2000, p. 1A).

This community mobilization for literacy—involving schools, parents, churches, businesses, and local groups—brought the community together around reading. The Reverend Franklyn Richardson, senior pastor of Grace Baptist Church, who was a trustee of the National Urban League as well as a leader of the community crusade to improve the schools, observed that district transformation cannot be achieved in the classroom alone; it requires conscious involvement by the wider community of parents, church leaders, and politicians ("The Mount Vernon Story," 2000).

The mobilization effort spearheaded by Superintendent Ross undoubtedly was a contributing factor in the striking surge in reading scores. In 1999, only 35 percent of Mount Vernon's 4th graders passed the New York State language arts exam. That rate jumped to 48 percent in 2000, soared again the following year to 74 percent, and reached 87 percent by 2005 (Mount Vernon City School District, 2006; Zernike, 2001).

In Mount Vernon's case, the reading competition was initiated and orchestrated by the school superintendent, but it could just as easily be spearheaded in other communities by school-based educators working in concert with community groups. Clearly, as was the case in Mount Vernon, creating incentives and stunts that spur youngsters to read of their own volition produces a win–win–win for the schoolchildren, their schools, and their teachers.

Conquering the SAT

The Urban League in Columbia, South Carolina, staged the most improbable mobilization initiative I have ever heard of. The organization joined forces with State Farm to mount an SAT awareness rally. It's hard to imagine an unlikelier drawing card than the dreaded SAT. When I first heard about this idea, I figured this was one happening that teenagers would avoid like the plague.

As J. T. McLawhorn, the CEO of the Columbia Urban League, recalls, the idea grew out of his conversation with Eleanor Horne, a vice president of the Educational Testing Service (ETS) and trustee of the National Urban League. They were discussing the fact that South Carolina students ranked last, or nearly so, in SAT scores. This performance was a source of embarrassment and defensiveness in the state, with some educators claiming that low-performing black students dragged down the state's scores. This view, in McLawhorn's opinion, created a stigma of inferiority among black youngsters.

So the Urban League decided to counteract it by staging the rally, whose theme was "Conquering the SAT." The simple goal was to demystify the SAT and overcome many students' anxiety about taking the test. The Urban League promoted the rally as an opportunity to learn how to prepare for and take the exam.

The event was held in December 1998 at Benedict College. The Urban League initially expected about 200 high school juniors and seniors to show up. But when it got word that many more were likely to come, it had to move the rally from the original venue to the chapel, which had greater seating capacity.

It turns out over 700 people attended the rally. Roughly 60 percent were students; the rest were parents and other adults. School buses arrived from all over the state, bringing youngsters from predominantly black districts in rural South Carolina where SAT scores were very low. The featured speaker was Eleanor Horne of the ETS, hardly a celebrity in the minds of adolescents. She explained why the SAT was important to the students' futures and how they could gear up to perform well on the test. The state commissioner of education addressed the audience as well, followed by a Q&A for the young people and their parents.

Horne brought practice tests in the verbal and math sections of the entrance exam, along with tips on test-taking do's and don'ts. These were the kinds of test-taking aids that children from wealthier families routinely receive from private tutorial outfits. The Urban League distributed these materials to the young people in attendance. One logistical problem that cropped up unexpectedly was that when the Urban League learned that so many youngsters were going to show up, it had to scramble to secure extra copies of the practice tests.

At the rally, some parents raised questions about whether the SAT is biased. If that's the case, they asked, why should their children bother to take it or even try to do well? Horne helped to overcome their skepticism by debunking the myth that it was impossible for black students to earn a good score on the exam. She demonstrated that with proper instruction and adequate time on task, children who are growing up in tough circumstances can improve their scores. Her remarks were empowering to parents and students who were wondering why they should bother.

The rally was a novelty as far as the news media was concerned. A couple of weeks prior to the rally, I attended a reception that McLawhorn hosted for local TV and radio station managers to try to convince them to cover the event. The press in Columbia took us up on our sales pitch. When the SAT rally occurred a couple of weeks later, it became the lead story of the evening newscasts on three television channels at 6 p.m. and 11 p.m., complete with live feeds from Benedict College to kick off the newscasts. Television screens were filled that night with the sight of the crowded chapel and images of energized black teenagers full of purpose. The youngsters told television reporters that they turned out because they understood that achievement is cool and because they were determined to get into college.

The Urban League secured a modest corporate contribution of $3,000 to help pay for the rally, while the college absorbed the cost of the chapel and security. (It helped that the president of Benedict chaired the board of the affiliate.) The SAT rally produced a dividend for the Columbia Urban League, which went on to secure a $35,000 grant from the state education agency to conduct SAT prep classes in three rural counties. Urban League officials say their students have registered an average 100-point gain on the exam.

Urban League affiliates in Columbia and elsewhere provide SAT tutorial courses, advice on how to apply to college and prepare the required essays, information about available scholarships and financial aid, and tours of college campuses. They also reach out directly to parents through workshops and op-ed articles. The Urban League's blunt message is that if youngsters do not succeed academically, then their parents should look in the mirror and partly blame themselves. It's their responsibility, the Urban League tells them, to make sure their child receives an adequate education. If parents accept inferior education, then parents are partly to blame. Parents must not take a backseat in the educational process.

Direct services like these may not fit the traditional mold of community mobilization. But they represent distinctive efforts to marshal the resources of community organizations to motivate youngsters to aim for college by helping them throughout the application process. The rally at Benedict College shows how reachable youngsters are when determined adults use their imaginations to spread the gospel of achievement.

Starting a Community-Based Honor Society

The centerpiece of the National Urban League's crusade to mobilize communities to spread the gospel of achievement was our community-based honor society, known as the National Achievers Society (NAS).

The National Honor Society is the gold standard when it comes to recognizing the academic achievements of schoolchildren. As a membership entity, it provides a prestigious peer group to which high achievers can belong. Yet the lofty standards and exclusivity that make it so special severely limit it as a means to motivate youngsters who are struggling academically or have "disidentified" with achievement. Shockingly few students in inner-city high schools ever qualify for admission. To reach and engage young people who aren't scholastic superstars, educators and communities need to create more accessible positive groups to which youngsters can belong—ones that honor a broad range of valued accomplishments.

This is precisely why Israel (Ike) Tribble, the late head of the Florida Education Fund, founded the McKnight Achievers Society in 1985 as a community-based vehicle for recognizing achievers and encouraging black children to do well in school. For over a decade, Urban League affiliates in the state collaborated with Tribble in inducting academic stars who had earned GPAs of 3.0 (equivalent to a B average) or better into this august body. It provided these young people with encouragement and, frankly, protective cover from peers who scorned both the idea of achievement and those who achieve.

Early in my tenure at the helm of the National Urban League, I attended an induction ceremony for the McKnight Achievers Society in Fort Lauderdale, Florida. The experience moved me because I saw first-hand that it is indeed possible to reach youngsters with our message that achievement matters. The Campaign for African-American Achievement embraced this concept of a community-based honor society and, with the enthusiastic backing of Tribble and the Urban League affiliates in Florida, took it national. Thus, in the spring of 1998, the National Urban League and the Congress of National Black Churches (the umbrella organization for the eight largest African American Christian denominations) launched a National Achievers Society for youngsters who do well in school.

The induction ceremonies have variously been described as gala occasions, community get-togethers, and feel-good affairs. Having participated in several, I can attest that they were all of that and then some. Because the inductions typically occurred in churches, the program included a solemn religious component, with invocations, prayers, and benedictions offered by the host pastors and visiting religious leaders.

Faithful to the original design of the McKnight Achievers Society, there were two categories of students affiliated with NAS. The so-called achievers already performed well in school, with a 3.0 GPA or better. Then there were the "believers." These students had at least a 2.5 GPA. They did not meet the threshold criteria for induction but were demonstrating sufficiently solid academic promise to be singled out for recognition at the induction ceremonies and exhorted to qualify for full-fledged induction in the near future. In other words, NAS aimed to celebrate achievers and motivate believers.

The first ceremony took place on April 17, 1998, at Metropolitan Baptist Church in Washington, D.C. Nationwide, 32 Urban League affiliates and their partners staged ceremonies inducting more than 2,000 young people between the ages of 5 and 17 (Shepard, 1998). Each year after, NAS staged a so-called flagship induction ceremony that set the pace for the Achievement Campaign and hopefully attracted national media attention. In a coup for the Achievement

Campaign, General Colin Powell graciously served as keynote speaker at the first flagship ceremony. The 35 inductees received designer jackets fashioned by Karl Kani, one of the hottest designers at the time in the eyes of young people. Echoing the military's training philosophy, Powell told the inductees, "There is nothing in this society you can't have. There is no job you can't have or profession you can't excel in. But you are going to have to work for it" (Shepard, 1998, para. 6). He added a poignant message to the adults in the audience: "We have seen so much progress in the 50 years since I was coming up. But it will all be irrelevant if we can't bring up this new generation of youngsters to believe in themselves" (para. 8).

I vividly recall the induction ceremony for the local chapter of the Achievers Society that was staged by the San Diego Urban League one Saturday afternoon in December at Bayview Baptist Church. The church was packed with 1,800 well-wishers rooting for the achievers. In fact, the audience overflowed to such a degree that some people had to sit onstage in the pews customarily occupied by the church choir.

Arrayed before us were 350 inductees, all of whom had earned *B* averages or better in school—*and half of whom were boys*. Judge Joe Brown, the television personality, was the keynote speaker. Interestingly enough, high school students who had previously been inducted into NAS played a major role in organizing the ceremony that day, and two of them served as emcees. Not only that, they kept the adult speakers on a tight leash time-wise.

The San Diego induction ceremony, and others like it, took place in a black church, and the event lasted much longer than the typical school period claimed by the school-based Honor Society. Between assembling the youngsters and audience, staging the ceremony itself, and holding the reception afterward, the festivities lasted close to three hours. In other words, this was no hit-and-run event. It was a very big deal to the schoolchildren, their families, and the many teachers who attended.

The *San Diego Voice & Viewpoint*, which is the local black newspaper, provided enthusiastic and extensive coverage of the induction ceremony. Starting on the front page, it devoted fully a dozen pages to text and photos of the inductees and their families ("National Urban League Honors Students," 2001). I was struck by the fact that not one of the inductees disparaged achievement as "acting white." They all eagerly stepped forward to be anointed as achievers and proudly wore the customized jackets available only to NAS members. Many kids I talked with there and at other ceremonies around the country asked what had taken the grown-ups so long to find them, to recognize them, and to provide them with the protective cover of a like-minded peer group.

The San Diego Urban League typically inducted between 250 and 600 students. The audience averaged two to three times that number. Its NAS events never drew fewer than 1,000 people. In recent years, the Urban League has staged the ceremonies outdoors at the Spreckels Organ Pavilion in Balboa Park. The event attracts lots of tourists, who get to see the hundreds of achievers on display. The cost of an induction ceremony ranges from less than $5,000 at a church to the $30,000 it once—and only once—cost to mount the ceremony in a hotel.

To reach and motivate the maximum number of students each year, the Urban League in Gary, Indiana, honored every youngster from grades 4 through 12 who earned a 3.0 GPA (or equivalent in the early grades). In 1998 alone, the Urban League inducted some 2,000 students. In contrast to some NAS chapters where achievers were inducted only once, the philosophy of this Urban League was "the more honorees, the merrier." It inducted youngsters the first time they earned a 3.0 GPA. But it also recognized them every year thereafter that they earned these grades. Another key to the vast number of honorees each year was the fact that the Urban League drew nominees not just from Gary but from all 15 school districts in the vicinity. At the end of the school year, it also honored the top 25 achievers from each of the high schools in these districts.

As with its big readathon, the Urban League in Gary drew on its long-standing collaborative relationships with the local school systems. There was no way the affiliate could carry off the Achievers Society, as the staff conceived it, without working closely and cooperatively with the schools. After all, it was up to the school systems to access their databases and identify every student who had earned a 3.0 GPA. The eligible children's teachers actually nominated them for induction and notified them and their parents of the prospective honor.

At the ceremony, the youngsters sat with their school contingents. Parents received a packet including a T-shirt, medallion, certificate, and NAS pin. To keep the costs manageable, the Urban League got the mayor of Gary to pay for the pins and persuaded a local printer to produce the program books pro bono. As should be no surprise given its imposing size, the annual induction ceremony in Gary attracted media attention from local newspapers and television stations.

The concept of the Achievers Society impressed John Modest, principal of Southeast Raleigh High School in Raleigh, North Carolina: "This is a win–win situation for the schools and the kids. It is an idea that is as simple as it is needed" (Simmons, 2001, p. 1B).

Public recognition in the company of so many fellow achievers unquestionably made a favorable impression on the inductees. As JaToya Jones, a high school freshman in Gary, remarked, "I was unaware of the amount of students coming here tonight. It's great that the Urban League is doing it, because it builds the students' self-esteem and makes us want to work harder in our studies" (DeNeal, 1998, p. B3). Amber Demerson Lewis, a high school senior who was inducted into NAS, echoed this sentiment: "I didn't know people were watching me and seeing that I was doing well in school. It made me feel really honored for people to recognize me" (Price, 1998).

Funding and Collaborators

Over the years, funding for carrying out the National Achievers Society has come from a variety of sources. In the early going, when several Urban League affiliates in Florida operated the predecessor program, the McKnight Achievers Society, they received $25,000 per year for this and related achievement-oriented programs from the Florida Education Fund, whose leader originated the achievers' program. Don Bowen, former CEO of the Broward County affiliate, recalls that this level of support was reasonably adequate at the outset. But as the scope and cost of the program grew, his affiliate was obliged to secure matching grants from the local United Way and eventually qualified for a five-year grant of $100,000 per annum from the National Urban League out of funds it received from the Lilly Endowment for the Achievement Campaign.

In some communities, parents paid a modest induction fee of, say, $50 that covered the jackets, certificates, and related costs. These fees were waived if necessary. Elsewhere, the local Urban League secured contributions from companies and other local sources to cover the cost. The National Urban League also obtained multiyear support from State Farm that enabled us to help affiliates with their local Achievement Campaigns, including the costs associated with operating NAS.

The National Achievers Society typically attracted an array of enthusiastic local collaborators. In Washington, D.C., for instance, these included the city's Parks Department, the Boys and Girls Clubs, the YWCA, and Reading Is Fundamental, as well as fraternities, sororities, and other civic-minded social groups. Elsewhere, one of the more unexpected sponsors was the Fort Wayne Philharmonic, which played classical music as accompaniment at the induction ceremony. Other sponsors across the country included local banks, public housing authorities, drug prevention agencies, and even math clubs in schools.

The Urban League in Broward County, Florida, encountered some financial pressure in conjunction with the program as revenue slipped and expenses crept up. It charged an induction fee of $60 that covered the jacket. The schools paid this fee out of discretionary funds for those whose families could not afford it. The Urban League also granted fee waivers and raised scholarship funds to help needy families. When the school system's discretionary resources shriveled up, it got fewer nominations for NAS. The induction ceremonies are held in black churches, which used to provide their facilities gratis. But now the Urban League must rent the space. All totaled, an induction event costs roughly $2,000.

Expanded Services

Urban League affiliates involved with the Achievement Campaign became convinced that more sustained activity was necessary to keep the issue of achievement front and center in the community (Academy for Educational Development [AED], 2005). Because recognizing these young people and celebrating their achievements builds social capital, those associated with the campaign felt a need to do this often and not just at specified times. Thus, by the fifth year of the Achievement Campaign, roughly half of the affiliates with NAS chapters were conducting two induction ceremonies a year. As one celebrant observed, "This gives the youth twice the joy, twice the encouragement, twice the support" (AED, 2005, p. 22).

The Broward County Urban League was among those staging two inductions annually, first in the fall and again in the spring. Initially, it inducted 150 to 200 youngsters during each round. But in recent years, the yield has declined to about 75 per session. Former CEO Don Bowen attributes this decrease to the imposition of more stringent standards. In addition to a 3.0 GPA, aspirants were required to submit an essay about why they wanted to belong to NAS. He believes that the added assignment may have turned off some youngsters.

Some affiliates that had the staff and financial wherewithal to do more than orchestrate the induction process offered additional services to the inductees. For example, the Houston Urban League preceded its NAS ceremony with an Academic Bowl Game for the inductees.

In Columbus, Ohio, the local Urban League offers an extensive menu of activities to keep NAS members engaged. As the Academy for Educational Development observes,

> Columbus has a chockfull, year long agenda of innovative, fun activities that include college tours, talent shows, science, math and reading camps and mentoring programs. The young people there described the non-stop activities at the Affiliate in very enthusiastic terms and said it was obvious that the Affiliate, and in particular the [Achievement Campaign] Coordinator cared about them, which made them want to participate. (2005, p. 38)

A Pro-achievement Peer Group

According to Kelly Price Noble, the former project coordinator and associate director of education at the San Diego Urban League, the NAS induction ceremonies were not hard to plan and pull off. The Urban League sent the selection criteria to school administrators so they would know whom to be on the lookout for. It reserved a church or hall for the ceremony itself. It operated a Thursday night group for students where they could discuss peer-group issues. These young-sters helped promote NAS by making phone calls, writing schools, and actually pushing academically eligible students to participate. These youngsters also ran the NAS induction ceremony and served as emcees.

In contrast to the reticence of the honor student described in Ron Suskind's 1994 *Wall Street Journal* article, NAS inductees eagerly stepped forward to be anointed as achievers. The Society provided young people with a critically important peer group that viewed academic achievement positively. As Chhabria Roberts, a senior at Homestead High School in Milwaukee who belonged to NAS, said of the image that achieving in school is tantamount to "acting white," "I brush it off, but it really hurts. How can you act like a color? I am speaking correct English, the same English that Booker T. Washington spoke, and Frederick Douglass" (Thomas-Lynn, 2006, para. 2). McKenzie Martin, a senior at Wauwatosa East High School and one of only two blacks out of 69 students inducted into her school's National Honor Society, captured the importance of NAS as a community-based alternative: "Whenever we meet, you see that you are not the only one" (Thomas-Lynn, 2006, para. 14).

The bottom line is that by virtue of creating their own mechanism for honoring achievement, the groups affiliated with the Achievement Campaign demonstrated that communities can be successfully mobilized to motivate youngsters to achieve. It can be done because, clearly, it *has* been done.

Looking back on the Achievement Campaign, I think fondly of the National Achievers Society as a nationwide "achievement gang," complete with its own rituals and regalia, credo, and colors. By deed and by word, these "gang" members transmitted a pro-achievement message to their peers. On my watch at the National

Urban League, we inducted over 25,000 members, including the 10,000 who had previously belonged to McKnight, into 35 NAS chapters around the country, thereby honoring them for their accomplishments while spreading the gospel of achievement to their siblings and buddies.

Clearly, the need and the opportunities to spawn community-based honor societies similar to NAS are vast, provided the goodwill, requisite collaboration, and modest resources can be marshaled on behalf of motivating youngsters to achieve. Although NAS is tethered to the Urban League, the idea of a community-based honor society is definitely worth emulating where the National Achievers Society does not exist.

Evaluating the Campaign

The Achievement Campaign mounted by the National Urban League serves as a tantalizing real-world example of the benefits that can accrue when educators and communities join forces to motivate youngsters to achieve. That the Urban League put achievement on the radar screens of young people, giving it credibility and cachet in kids' eyes, was affirmed by the AED, which conducted an assessment of the Campaign for African-American Achievement. AED (2005) notes in its evaluation:

> The most striking finding is that the Campaign fills a long unmet need for recognition on the part of young African Americans who excel academically. In contrast to peers who may be celebrated for their athletic prowess, "smart" youth have often been the butt of jokes and ridicule and their treatment at the hands of their peers has further reinforced the myth that it is not "cool" to be smart. (p. 34)

The AED report continues:

NAS (National Achievers Society), Achievement Month, and Doing the Right Thing Celebrations partially remediate this situation by saluting young people for their academic efforts. The impact of this cannot be underestimated. Focus group respondents actually marveled at the turn of events whereby their peers were seeking them out to find out how "to get one of those jackets." (p. 34)

The young people who were reached by the Achievement Campaign cited a number of benefits, notably a clearer sense of what it means to achieve:

In the materialistic culture in which all of these youth live, many acknowledged that their peers and even they, themselves, defined achievement in strictly material terms, focusing on short-term gain. However, participation in the Campaign has helped to change these perceptions. Coupled with this clearer understanding of achievement is also a clearer sense of how academic achievement and future success are linked. Young people report that exposure to the Campaign is implanting and reinforcing the message that regardless of the career path they choose to pursue, academic achievement will make it easier. (AED, 2005, pp. 34–35)

The AED evaluators also report glowingly on the Urban League's community-based honor society:

The National Achievers Society helped to establish a common bond among young people in the same community but not necessarily of the same background. Within the same focus groups, participants often hailed from disparate backgrounds. However, the quest to achieve united them. They spoke of the positive peer influence that they exerted on each other as one of the benefits of the Campaign. They also mentioned how collectively they are changing the often negative perception of African American youth in their communities. (2005, p. 36)

AED praises the Urban League affiliates for helping the nonachievers in their communities:

Many of the affiliates . . . have started Believers groups for individuals whose GPA is not sufficiently high to allow them membership in the Achievers Society. The youth in question and their parents and teachers note that this is very important because in some cases these youth have felt marginalized as all of the attention is focused on youth who are excelling. The Believers groups promote the philosophy that the community believes that these young people, with extra effort, can become tomorrow's Achievers. The establishment of the Believers groups has gone a long way to dispelling the notion that the NAS is an exclusionary group. (p. 38)

The youngsters reached by the Achievement Campaign saw the assistance they received with practical problems as another dividend. Many of the communities that Urban League affiliates serve suffer from a dearth of useful information about how to get ahead, especially in school. The children and parents who have been involved in the campaign cited the information they had received on college applications, scholarships, tutoring, and job placement as particularly helpful. This assistance extended to nonacademic concerns, too, like money, time management, and even dress and grooming. The young people also welcomed the support they received from the caring adults on the affiliate staffs and among the members of the partnering groups involved.

Now that the idea of mobilizing communities to motivate youngsters to achieve is no longer an abstraction but a set of real-world examples, the next chapter provides practical guidance for educators about how to galvanize communities to bring about these benefits for students.

Ways to Promote Academic Success

- Stage events year-round that champion achievement.
- Encourage and support community partners to plan and lead achievement-boosting activities so that they genuinely embrace achievement as "their" issue.
- As commitment to the cause builds, introduce new activities commensurate with the expanded support and capacity.
- Foster the establishment of community-based honor societies as a way for the broad community to "own" achievement.
- Seek funding for out-of-pocket costs, but be careful not to trigger a funding race among community partners.
- Establish a credible mechanism to monitor implementation and assess impact.

5

MOBILIZING THE VILLAGE

How does the process of mobilizing the community get started? I believe the best way to begin is with a low-key meeting, hosted by the local school superintendent (preferably in conjunction with the head of the school board) with invitations extended to a small cross section of business and community leaders as well as representatives of the public library system. If the size of the school system makes a single districtwide strategy impractical, the superintendent might focus on reaching out to leaders in those neighborhoods where low achievement is most pervasive and persistent and the need to motivate students is most acute.

The kinds of groups to invite to an initial mobilization meeting like this are those with a reputation for genuinely caring about children's education and with a track record of playing constructive roles toward that end. This is a conversation and an enterprise for serious organizations only. Although the roster of potential players will clearly vary by community, the cast might include respected social services, civil rights and youth services organizations, civic-minded business groups, social and fraternal organizations that sponsor youth-related projects, and religious leaders who have demonstrated that they're already solidly on the achievement page and doing something concrete about it.

I generally believe in taking the path of least resistance, so I would counsel against inviting organizations that aren't already involved in education and youth development for the simple reason that it might take too much explaining and persuading to get them up to speed. At the outset it is wiser to forge coalitions composed of a cadre of highly respected groups that really get the point of the enterprise. Once the coalition and its agenda solidify, other groups can be incorporated, provided they are willing to embrace the fundamental game plan and carry their weight.

At the initial gathering, school officials could explain that the meeting has two purposes. The first is to brief those in attendance on the school district's near-term and long-term plans for boosting student achievement across the board and especially where the need for progress is most pressing. The superintendent might then go on to say, with disarming candor, that the second purpose is to signal that the schools and educators in the system cannot possibly succeed on their own. If children who aren't faring well in school develop a stronger desire to do well, then it will be easier for educators to reach them, teach them, and thus enable them to learn and achieve. The schools need help from parents and community groups in persuading youngsters to want to learn and do well in school.

Toward that end, the superintendent's message might continue, the school district is eager to enter into a strategic partnership with the leading community groups that genuinely care about children to jointly plan and implement a series of year-round activities designed to motivate children to achieve. After some discussion of these opening topics, the superintendent or a member of her or his team could briefly describe the kinds of activities (such as those covered in this book) that have been mounted successfully in other school districts. The point of these examples is to further community leaders' investment in the initiative and thus inspire them to begin envisioning what could be done in their town, rather than have school officials "decree" what is going to be done.

This initial meeting should conclude with the superintendent explaining the next steps—the formation of a steering committee with the straightforward mission to design and orchestrate the multi-faceted, community-based effort to motivate youngsters to achieve—and eliciting commitments to serve on this committee from as many of the attending groups as are willing to join in. School officials should be mindful that some representatives of these groups, especially volunteer organizations, may need to secure authorization from their membership before the group can commit to be involved.

The superintendent should serve ex officio on the committee, along with a senior staffer who reports directly to the superintendent and an active member of the committee. Absent school district engagement from the very top, the steering committee will lack the entrée and clout to secure the cooperation from every level of the school district that is needed to ensure the successful operation and hoped-for impact of the motivational activities.

Ideally, this steering committee composed of educators and community and business leaders would coalesce around a series of strategically timed and sequenced events (such as those described in this book or variations thereof) that keep children's attention riveted on achievement year-round. In formulating its action plan, the committee will undoubtedly bat around the kinds of ideas described in this book and others that occur to them. They should also discuss the need to transmit this message via a series of events and activities, instead of trying it once and hoping the message sticks.

Lastly, they should devise a preliminary game plan that includes the kinds of activities to be mounted; the specific cooperation needed from the superintendent and school board, the central administration, and participating schools in the district; the potential contributions that various kinds of groups can make; the organizations that should be enlisted for their ideas and involvement; and the financial and human resources that will be needed to pull this off. Another important decision is how many activities, and specifically which ones, should be launched in the first year and which ones should be brought onboard going forward (and at what pace). This steering committee should also determine how the initiative will be orchestrated, including the designation of one organization to function as the secretariat and fiscal agent. Once the initial steering committee gets its sea legs, so to speak, the members should determine whether its composition is well suited for the long haul. As the group morphs into a permanent steering committee, it may be wise for it to recruit additional members who possess the stature, connections, constituent base, and clout to command respect and help carry out this initiative.

Once a preliminary list and sequence of activities are identified, then the steering committee might want to create planning subcommittees for each of the initiatives. These subcommittees could take the ball and run with it, provided they agree to coordinate with the others in terms of theme and timing.

In addition to having the superintendent's designee as an active member, the steering committee should periodically brief the school superintendent and school board on its evolving agenda and upcoming activities. They obviously should also seek the advice and ideas, as well as the cautions, of these school district leaders in order to ensure that the expectations of the school district and the community remain synchronized every step of the way and that the district continues to back the mobilization effort with genuine enthusiasm. For if the school district and steering committee drift apart and start to work at cross purposes, the initiative will sputter, everyone will become frustrated, and the innocent bystanders—namely, the schoolchildren—will be shortchanged.

In addition to planning and implementing the events, the steering committee could try to enlist leaders with platforms and megaphones, if you will, who are willing to tout the importance of literacy and achievement. Leaders of this ilk include pastors, radio talk show hosts, local newspaper columnists, elected officials, local entertainers, heads of activist groups, and so forth. They should be asked to join in pushing the achievement message and promoting the motivational events.

In conjunction with this initiative, a concerted effort should be made to engage community organizations and faith-based institutions with sizable constituencies, deep roots, and routine weekly or monthly connections with their members. In particular, there should be an emphasis on PTAs, block clubs, and women's service clubs and sororities like Eastern Star, the Links, and Deltas. Men's organizations like the Elks, Masons, fraternities, and service clubs should be sought out as well. Efforts could be made to blanket residences, community groups, beauty parlors, barbershops, and neighborhood stores with flyers that promote the achievement events and lay out what parents and caregivers need to know and can do.

Velma Cobb, who spearheaded the Achievement Campaign for the National Urban League, stresses the importance of partners. She told me that no single community group should try to dominate the mobilization agenda, lest the other groups begin to feel like appendages, not partners. If the partners genuinely share ownership, then they better understand what needs to be done and why.

Smaller partners may be easier to work with than bigger ones, because there are fewer conflicts over agendas, and they feel less need to claim credit or assert leadership. Cobb noted that Urban League affiliates forged strong relationships with small churches and small community groups that serve children. When invited to play a role and offered clear, practical information about how to proceed, small churches and groups are often pleased to collaborate.

Navigating Challenges

For educators, forging and sustaining partnerships with community groups presents some challenges. After all, educators already have their hands full trying to motivate and teach the children. Plus, collaborating with community groups usually isn't part of their job description, let alone the curricula at schools of education. There may have been tensions between the schools and the community in times past. But working with partners is essential if educators are to mobilize the community.

Recruiting Fellow Educators

One challenge for educators who want to lead the charge in working with community groups is to recruit their colleagues to the cause. After all, educators are very busy people. School officials sometimes were simply too busy to get involved in the Achievement Campaign. Local Urban Leagues also experienced some difficulty in persuading schools to identify eligible students and getting the students to complete the necessary paperwork for induction. Moreover, fewer school officials knew about the mission and purpose of the effort than would have been expected, given its focus and the potential benefit to the schools.

The superintendent can always decree that the schools will collaborate with the community mobilization effort. But I'm convinced that the key to recruiting school officials, particularly teachers and principals on the front lines, and securing their enthusiastic involvement is to help them understand why these community-based efforts to motivate children to achieve are in educators' professional self-interest. Their job is easier when youngsters want to do well in school. And student motivation, in turn, helps boost the performance of the schools.

Another concern for educators is turnover at the central office and building levels. Superintendents come and go these days with destabilizing frequency. Approaches that are embraced by one superintendent may need to be sold afresh to successors who are determined to implement their own ideas. School-based personnel may be in constant flux as well, so that contacts made one year may need to be cultivated anew the next year. One answer for educators who spearhead efforts to mobilize the community is to nurture at least two liaisons at all participating schools to ensure continuity of cooperation if one of them leaves.

Working with Volunteer Groups

Volunteer civic, social, and fraternal groups bring many assets to the enterprise, including membership, contacts, and cachet. But they can be tricky to collaborate with because of leadership rotations that mean their presidents typically serve for only two years. Although it is important to be mindful of the way these groups are structured, I hasten to add that many Urban Leagues across the country routinely collaborate with and rely on groups like these as partners because of the values and volunteer horsepower that they can bring to any undertaking that they embrace. Indeed, it is hard to imagine trying to undertake the kinds of mobilization efforts recommended in this book without relying on volunteer groups like these as enthusiastic and fully engaged partners.

Working with Churches

A particularly important dimension of any sustained campaign is to enlist churches to do their part for the children in their congregations. Ask pastors to promote literacy and achievement from the pulpit at designated intervals during the year. They might mobilize church members to monitor the literacy levels and academic performance of children in the church. In addition, they should ensure that young-sters enrolled in their own preschool and Sunday school programs are proficient readers and that the teachers in these programs tout achievement. Churches can stage literacy festivals and math or science fairs that are synchronized with other efforts in the community.

Despite these potential advantages, collaborating with churches and faith-based groups poses its own set of challenges. One experienced observer stated, "The churches have their own agendas, and the leaders are often reluctant to engage their members in external initiatives" (AED, 2005, p. 44). As AED notes in its report, the key to successful partnerships with religious groups appears to lie in convincing them that the partnerships are mutually beneficial to the church and to the campaign.

Those Urban League affiliates that enjoyed the greatest success in enlisting religious partners considered the needs of their respective religious organizations carefully before broaching the topic of a partnership. They then revisited these needs periodically once the partnership was launched. For instance, collaborations forged in conjunction with the Achievement Month/Doing the Right Thing activities that recognized youth members of the partnering congregations appeared to be an effective way to leverage church support (AED, 2005).

As a result of this kind of assiduous cultivation, the local clergy in Pittsburgh signed on to begin using their Sunday sermons to spread the gospel that achievement matters. In Colorado Springs, the religious partners supported the annual education summit. The CEO of the Louisville Urban League sold the school superintendent on the idea of having a dozen or so churches sponsor reading programs. The superintendent invited the Urban League to submit a proposal. That resulted in a $50,000 grant for the Shining Stars reading enrichment program. Operating in collaboration with the churches, this program enabled reading resource teachers to train tutors, who in turn worked with 50 students over the summer (AED, 2005). In other words, the basic challenge is to convince religious leaders that the vision and mission of mobilizing communities to motivate kids to achieve mesh with the vision and mission of the church or faith-based organization.

Working with Corporations

Corporate partnerships hold the promise of bringing valued financial and in-kind resources to any mobilization effort. State Farm was a highly visible and engaged partner to the National Urban League and many of its affiliates in their local Achievement Campaigns. Local offices of State Farm made financial and in-kind contributions and supplied staff as volunteers at events. The company also paid for advertising for the Doing the Right Thing festivals. It provided backpacks and supplies to participants who attended the annual back-to-school rally and education summits in Kansas City. What's more, State Farm representatives sat on the campaign steering committee. Indeed, the company played a major role in the sustainability plans of many affiliates.

But cultivating these relationships takes vision, clarity, diligence—and determination to deliver results. Remember that corporate partners want to see tangible results from their support. (In fact, they often serve as volunteers and provide additional in-kind support so that they can be close to the action.) This concern is understandable. After all, many corporate partners have to file reports to their supervisors, even to their boards of directors, on the outcomes of their corporate giving. The more involved partner staff members are in the collaboration, the easier it is for them to identify real outcomes and report on the tangible results of the partnership (AED, 2005).

Taking Action

The experiences of Urban League affiliates involved in the Achievement Campaign generated many lessons for educators who may want to mobilize their own communities to motivate students to achieve. Here is some advice derived from learning by doing.

Be Adaptable

There is no cookie-cutter approach to community mobilization and engagement. The circumstances of people, organizations, and communities vary considerably from one place to the next, even within the same neighborhood. For educators, the keys are patience and the capacity to listen and learn so that the strategies they craft are derived from reality and attuned to the community's dreams. Because the cast of key players occasionally shifts midstream, the strategies must be flexible enough and the roles must be fungible enough to accommodate these changes.

Give Volunteers a Clear Objective

Many community-based programs lack an organizational centerpiece to ground them. Volunteer groups that collaborate with schools often are not very structured. It is essential to harness and channel this volunteer energy. People and groups need to be galvanized around something concrete, and they require a strategy, tools, and resources to drive toward the desired outcome. Clarity of objective and outcomes sought is crucial because nonprofit groups often struggle to establish and strive for desired results. At the end of the day, these collaborative efforts must be able to demonstrate value added and show that the effort and resources they marshaled produced results—for example, by shifting the attitudes of parents and children toward literacy and achievement.

Think Long-Term

Avoid one-shot activities. Whatever is undertaken should be an integral part of an overarching strategy designed to improve children's literacy and scholastic performance.

Act Locally

One indispensable lesson that recurred throughout the Achievement Campaign was that it is difficult to drive this agenda on a "wholesale" basis—that is, through national membership organizations that have their own institutional imperatives and priorities. What's more, many national volunteer outfits rotate their leaders every few years, which makes it tough to sustain their commitment to agendas that aren't already deeply rooted in the organization. Instead, it appears to be more effective to "go retail," so to speak, by enlisting collaborators locally, community by community, church by church.

Enlist the Media

The varied events that I have described in this book are naturals for the news media, from conventional outlets to local cable newscasts and school district channels, shoppers' newspapers, church bulletins, the Web, and other nontraditional outlets that reach people. Call upon the media to underscore your message that student achievement matters to the community.

Cultivate Relationships

Relationships and personal contacts with the schools were very important to the success of the National Achievers Society. In Broward County, Florida, it helped greatly that the Urban League's part-time education director—the person principally responsible for the achievers' program—was a longtime, full-time teacher in the local school system. As a native of Broward County, she knew key people in the school system and how to get them to cooperate and support NAS. In particular, she knew the guidance counselors, who had to nominate kids for induction, and understood how to get them to pay attention to notices and respond to requests for nominees. When this director assumed other assignments at the affiliate, her replacements were not as effective because they lacked roots in the schools and the community.

As with many community efforts, all may not be smooth sailing in every neighborhood and during every phase of planning and implementation. AED's (2005) assessment notes that sites with National Achievers Societies had varying levels of difficulty in getting schools to identify eligible students and getting the students to complete the necessary paperwork for induction. Strategies that proved effective in overcoming these challenges were (1) establishing and maintaining a close working relationship with school superintendents so that they advocate for and publicize the programs among the schools; (2) establishing and maintaining a close working relationship with school counselors, who have access to grade reports and can therefore determine which students are eligible; and (3) advertising the program directly to youth so that they can pressure their schools to release the necessary information.

Use Committees and Teams to Divide Labor

To help solicit names of eligible students, orchestrate NAS, and organize the induction ceremonies, the San Diego Urban League created a United Front and Family Resource Support Network. Composed of about 15 community groups, this steering committee would send letters soliciting nominations to a wide array of organizations, among them the Baptist Ministries, NAACP, and black sororities and fraternities.

The steering committee divvied up the tasks among different clusters of member groups. It established as many as 15 teams. The NAS induction ceremony itself was organized by representatives of the Urban League's youth leadership teams, the NAACP, and other groups. Other committee members dealt with logistics, promotion, and program setup. Parents pitched in as well. The steering committee's philosophy was that it had roles for anyone who wanted to help, and it welcomed people to contribute however they were able to.

Encourage Student Participation

Jimma McWilson, the former director of the Achievement Campaign at the San Diego Urban League, made certain that youngsters played a major role in the National Achievers Society. Instead of dominating the action, staff and parents became coaches who stayed out of sight. The students were the key players in holding the induction ceremonies. They planned the event, conducted their own research on the speakers, and wrote their own remarks. At every ceremony, a female and male student teamed up as co-emcees.

Keep the Focus on Children

McWilson cites several challenges in running NAS and mounting the induction ceremonies. One of the biggest problems he faced was keeping organizations composed of adults focused on the children instead of on adult needs and issues. Adult issues kept cropping up, such as how the grown-ups intended to promote themselves and their groups. Keeping adults on task was one of the hardest tasks.

In fact, the challenges of keeping adults in community groups on task has led McWilson in his most recent work to concentrate first on families, which in turn are focused on their children. It is his experience that poor people bring amazing resources to the table. In working with community parents, he cautions, it is important to speak in positive tones. Badgering them simply turns them off to the message. What's more, he works with organizations through the parents who belong to them, not via their leaders. He gets relatives of the children to reach out to the people they know in organizations and churches. That is the way, he maintains, to get the people who are involved and invested in the church to take lead responsibility.

Don't Rely Too Heavily on Financial Resources

Interestingly enough, a couple of college professors took issue with the "50 books and a bike" effort. They argued that children should not be bribed with bicycles to read. Their skepticism echoes a practical concern about the sustainability of efforts that rely on rather expensive incentives. In fact, the following year Superintendent Ross hoped to award free laptops to the winners. But he could not generate enough donations to proceed with the idea.

Involve the Local Churches

The San Diego Urban League enjoyed considerable success in getting local black churches engaged with NAS. As Jimma McWilson recounts it, that is because he viewed them as a mini-village. For instance, he typically asked the churches which youngsters they thought were doing the right thing. In response, the pastor would identify the children and their parents who fit the criteria. The church supplied the names of the schoolchildren in its congregation who were on the honor roll. The Urban League verified this information by requiring parents to go to school and get written validation. This approach in turn connected the parents with the schools.

In other words, McWilson always started with the church, which he calls the inner community. The so-called outer community needs to see that the inner community is committed. Next, the Urban League broadened the concentric circle of involved groups by sending letters to black sororities and fraternities, many of which had heard about the Achievement Campaign through their churches.

Take Chances

A gifted community organizer when it comes to promoting achievement, Jimma McWilson also urges educators, especially principals, not to be afraid of the unknown or to be wary of bad experiences. As the CEO of the school building, principals have power that they can use to encourage parents to become the best resource network for their children and the schools.

Partnering for Success

Beyond the particular challenges posed by involving various types of partners, generic issues arise across the board that need to be addressed along the way. To begin with, partnerships tend to falter when there isn't a clearly articulated vision of how the proposed collaboration will support the campaign's mission, with a spelled-out sense of the respective roles of the partners. Problems can arise in working with local branches of national partners when the various parties are unclear as to the role of the local branches.

As collaborations move into the operational phase, insufficient consultation among partners can cause some organizations to lose interest. When partners are kept out of the loop, the partnership may suffer. According to AED (2005), reconciling the differing mandates of partnering groups represents yet another challenge for campaign partnerships.

Educators who endeavor to partner with nonprofit community groups, corporations, and religious institutions must face the fact that each has distinct mandates and operating principles. Corporations typically want to see quantitative outcomes. Religious organizations may be more concerned with the overall impact of a partnership on the spirituality and well-being of their congregations. The challenge for educators is to provide partners with the mutual understanding and support needed to stay active in the partnership. The lead community-based partner needs to be proactive and flexible in diagnosing and responding to partner needs.

To prevent confusion, disappointment, and wasted effort, partners also need to be explicit and consistent about what is expected of each party. If a group of educators takes the lead, it should not be shy about expressing its needs to prospective partners. By the same token, if the enterprise is truly a collaborative effort, then the mutual expectations and division of labor should be articulated so that roles and responsibilities are clear. In addition, the partners should meet periodically during the year to review expectations and ensure that all parties are still on the same page.

Mobilization efforts should concentrate on communicating clearly, consistently, and repeatedly to partners about the goals, objectives, and expected outcomes. As AED (2005) finds, when well-intentioned stakeholders who were critically important were only vaguely familiar with the specific aspects of a campaign and unclear about their roles, they did not perform as expected. Or they lost interest over time, some to the point of withdrawing completely. To facilitate communication, some Urban League affiliates actually prepared memoranda of understanding with partners. These formal agreements fostered an increased sense of ownership among partners.

A really effective—indeed, indispensable—way of keeping partners enthusiastically engaged is by establishing and maintaining contact between their representatives and the young people who benefit. AED (2005) observes that the experience of collaborating is more meaningful and gratifying to partners when they actually have regular contact with the ultimate beneficiaries of partnerships. Corporate partners—in fact, most partners—want a larger role than merely signing checks and attending a few planning meetings each year. They want to be actively involved and witness firsthand the difference they are making in the attitudes, academic performance, and lives of young people. Educators have the power to make this contact between community partners and students happen.

Recognizing Those Who Serve

Over the years, I have attended gala dinners aplenty that pay tribute to civic leaders, companies, and community groups that have improved the lives of young people, fostered equal opportunity, spurred the revitalization of struggling neighborhoods, or made other uplifting contributions to their communities. Yes, these events often double as fund-raisers for the sponsoring organization. But the recognition bestowed on those who serve affirms their value and spurs them on.

To stoke and sustain the energy that community group members, many of them volunteers, must muster to rise to this challenge and stay the course, it makes common sense to shower them with recognition and appreciation, just as we should the children who do the right thing. When you think about it, those shops that sell customized trophies and plaques would quickly go out of business if we were to suddenly stop celebrating the volunteers who log countless hours for noble causes. Hotels and banquet halls would suffer mightily if groups were to stop recognizing volunteers who purchase tables at gala dinners for family members, friends, and coworkers. Manufacturers of display cases and bookshelves would hurt financially if winners didn't need a prominent place to show off their prizes.

To galvanize community energy on behalf of achievement, I could imagine high-profile gala ceremonies staged annually at the local and state levels where groups that have successfully turned kids on to literacy and achievement receive coveted awards for their efforts. Modest cash grants or symbolic prizes might be given for the "best in class" in various categories. Examples might include churches and other faith-based programs; sororities and other women's organizations; fraternities, fraternal orders, and other men's groups; civic groups; youth services agencies; community-based organizations (CBOs) like local Urban Leagues and NAACP chapters; grassroots outfits like tenant associations; and business groups like the Lions and Rotary Clubs. The more the merrier.

These awards should be synchronized with the kinds of activities suggested earlier. For instance, there could be a category of awards for community groups involved in staging Literacy Olympiads and other activities aimed at encouraging reading. Another category might cover churches and faith-based groups that do a terrific job of promoting reading by young people in the church. Other awards could go to groups that collaborate in staging achievement fairs and Achievement Day parades, create "achievement gangs," and so forth. There could be recognition as well for organizations that come up with innovative new ways of motivating youngsters to achieve, whether it's an SAT rally one year or a mass readathon the next.

These ceremonies could be held at city hall, the state capitol, or a convention center. Come to think of it, why stop there? The recognized groups might go on to compete for highly coveted national awards that are presented at a gala national ceremony akin to the Academy Awards or the Kennedy Center Honors. Perhaps the ceremony could be telecast, carried on cable, or Webcast. Celebrities could present the awards accompanied by heartwarming video vignettes prior to each award. Admittedly, this last idea could be costly, but some education-minded advertisers might embrace it.

Thus, although it might seem corny, a proven way to galvanize and sustain community energy is to bathe the volunteers and staffers who rise to the occasion in recognition. Celebrating them will pay surefire dividends for the children they inspire to achieve.

Getting the Word Out

Another critically important segment of the community that should be mobilized is the media in its many forms. The cause of motivating youngsters to achieve can be aided enormously by a concerted media campaign to "sell" achievement to students and families. Another important audience is the collection of community groups that need to be mobilized.

In fact, an integral component of the Urban League's Achievement Campaign was its determined effort to market the message that "Achievement Matters" every way we could think of. Some messages and methods were geared explicitly to black parents, caregivers, and children. Other, more generic tactics targeted whomever we could reach.

State Farm partnered in this effort by purchasing advertisements in black newspapers that promoted our message. In addition to securing media coverage of their achievement-oriented events, many Urban League affiliates got really creative about communicating the achievement message. Some of them placed public service spots on radio and cable television. The Cincinnati Urban League persuaded local cinemas to carry "screen savers" with our message just before the previews of coming attractions. In Seattle, the municipal buses carried placards bearing the message that achievement matters.

The Urban League in Columbus, Ohio, enjoyed some success in attracting media interest. Instead of relying on the mainstream media to respond favorably to press releases, the affiliates started cultivating the media early in the year and began lining up media partners no later than four weeks prior to its events. A specific staff member was charged with this responsibility. As a result, their local campaign consistently garnered coverage (AED, 2005).

The Urban League in Houston understood the power of celebrity to convey its message. It recruited the four major sports teams in town—the Astros, Comets, Rockets, and Texans—to lend their support, thereby ensuring that the affiliate succeeded in penetrating an already oversaturated media market. By contrast, the Miami Urban League found that grassroots approaches—word of mouth and peer networks—were effective and kept media and marketing costs to a minimum. It produced its own flyers, brochures, and marketing materials and solicited donations from partners for printing and other services that could not be managed in-house (AED, 2005).

At the other end of the continuum, the Urban League in Gary, Indiana, used billboards to promote its *Read and Rise* initiative. The CEO of the affiliate approached LaMar Advertising, which owns billboards all around Gary and its environs. She told them that the Urban League wanted to make a really big deal of *Read and Rise* by plastering its message on billboards around town. LaMar responded favorably and donated space on 10 billboards, including a couple of large ones adjacent to the freeway. The billboards stayed up for two years.

Thus, Urban League affiliates involved in the Achievement Campaign used many different techniques to engage the media and spread the message that achievement matters. They became increasingly sophisticated about marketing achievement as their local Achievement Campaigns matured. As AED (2005) notes in its assessment, fiscal considerations drove most affiliates to use their contacts and leverage along with low-cost approaches like flyers and door-to-door solicitations to spread the word.

Despite these efforts, some affiliates complained of the lack of interest shown by major television and print media outlets in the Achievement Campaign. As one frustrated campaign partner said, "They [the media] seem very interested when there's something bad to report in our community—a shooting, a murder. But not when we are celebrating the achievements of our young people" (AED, 2005, pp. 24–25).

To understand the view from the other side, AED interviewed media organizations that actually did partner in the Achievement Campaign in 15 communities. Their responses were illuminating and instructive. They cited those circumstances under which the Achievement Campaign would likely generate coverage:

• *Long-standing relationship with the local Urban League that predates the campaign.* They added that if the affiliate waited until the campaign began to cultivate the media, this was certainly too late to be effective, at least in the first couple of years, if not over the entire course of the campaign.

• *Interest in education.* Some media outfits had an interest in education and were more likely to cover the Achievement Campaign. If the issue of education reform was considered newsworthy to them, then the campaign would likely attract some coverage.

• *Desire to fulfill FCC public service obligations.* All radio and TV stations are required to air a certain number of public service announcements. Savvy affiliates could exploit this requirement and work with media outfits to receive free or low-cost publicity.

Many educators are naturals when it comes to interacting with the news media: completely at ease and self-possessed in front of the camera or talking with reporters. They know how to prepare themselves for encounters with the press. They have a solid grasp of the story line they want to communicate, and they know instinctively how to avoid pitfalls and traps that interviewers may try to set. Even so, it never hurts to seek media training or a refresher course in press relations. Having worked as an editorial writer for the *New York Times* and an executive in public television, I was brimming with self-confidence when I took the helm of the National Urban League. Nevertheless, I underwent media training, and it paid off in dealing with an increasingly skeptical press and 24-hour cable TV and radio news outlets with plenty of airtime and a penchant for spotlighting the weaknesses of their guests.

Another lesson it took me a while to learn is that however important I may think our story is, the media marches to an entirely different drummer in terms of what they deem newsworthy. So it's important and pays off—at least some of the time—to try to figure out what kinds of stories will interest them, how to frame stories and events to attract the media's attention, what kinds of evidence and statistics are necessary to give an education story gravitas, and, from a defensive perspective, what kinds of foibles automatically attract their attention.

Assiduous cultivation of the media often pays dividends. When I wrote editorials for the *New York Times* in the late 1970s and early

1980s, Frank Macchiarola, the chancellor of the New York City schools, was masterful at cultivating the press. He and his press aide paid occasional visits just to keep us abreast of evolving developments in the school district, even when they weren't particularly seeking press coverage. Needless to say, they were all over us whenever they launched a new education initiative or had to cope with a high-profile crisis in the schools. If ever I needed to talk with Macchiarola, he quickly returned my calls or made himself available for a meeting. In other words, they built a relationship characterized by candor, access, and understanding that, I must confess in hindsight, probably took off a little bit of the edge if ever we needed to be strongly critical of the school system's actions or the chancellor's performance. Viewed from an educator's vantage point, that's effective media relations.

Probably the most enduring lesson from my many years of dealing with the media is that in the era of modern communications technology, there are multiple ways for educators to get the word out about what they and their students are doing. The more exasperated I got over the years trying to secure coverage for the National Urban League in the conventional media, the more determined I became to use the myriad forms of media out there and the new technologies like the Internet that were rapidly becoming available.

These technologies liberated us from the traditional gatekeepers who determined whether they would allow our story to reach interested audiences using their mode of transmission. Using the Internet, we could transmit right away, and we were left with the marketing challenge of letting potentially interested audiences know where to find our information. For example, we would Webcast plenary sessions, workshops, and press conferences from the Urban League's annual convention. Some events were carried live and repeated later; others that weren't time-sensitive were videotaped and transmitted later at considerably less expense. In other words, we created our own Internet-based network and also used the Web to spread the word to audiences, from laymen to policymakers and their staffs, who tended to be interested in our work and in what we had to say about the issues of the day.

Public access channels and local cable newscasts are another mechanism for reaching audiences. The Urban League also sought coverage in unconventional print vehicles, such as newsletters and magazines geared to members of volunteer organizations and church denominations. None of these alternatives can substitute for obtaining coverage in the highly watched mainstream news outlets, but they at least provide an alternative to getting frozen out entirely. As citizens gravitate increasingly to Internet sources of information, and as the Web becomes even more robustly interactive, 21st century technology will afford creative educators more and more ways to exploit so-called narrowcasting to reach their desired audiences.

To help spread the word about local mobilization activities, particular attention should be paid to recruiting prominent local radio talk show hosts who have a social conscience coupled with hours of airtime to fill daily. They can turn a cause into a personal crusade and champion the issue. Mainstream, minority, and community newspapers, even shoppers' papers, are other important vehicles for reaching people.

Modern telecommunications tools like cell phones and the Internet can be used to drum up interest and audiences for the events that are implemented in conjunction with the mobilization effort. These instant and ubiquitous means of communication have been marshaled in recent years to organize massive rallies on behalf of all manner of causes the world over. These methods can be deployed on behalf of achievement.

In addition to cause-related commercials and advertisements, educators and their partners can try some other wrinkles that reach families right where they live. I have in mind blanketing entire neighborhoods—beauty parlors and barbershops, clinics and doctors' offices, Head Start and child care centers—with leaflets and pamphlets that promote achievement and contain practical tips about what adults can do. What about placing stories in church bulletins and other in-house communication vehicles?

In conjunction with the marketing campaign, talking points could be prepared and offered to ministers for possible use in sermons and Sunday school. The same could be done for the heads of membership organizations whose meetings lean heavily on ritual.

The foregoing ideas are drawn from my Urban League experience and probably qualify as more opportunistic than strategic. Ideally, local groups should enlist expert marketers to craft a multifaceted campaign that saturates the airwaves, newspapers, and streets with captivating messages that move beyond touting a cause to closing the sale in the minds of youngsters and their parents. The key to any strategy is to conduct a reconnaissance of all the ways that community leaders, ordinary folks, and young people transmit and receive messages about what matters to them and moves them to act. Those "transmission belts," if you will, should be used to convey this message that is so vital to the viability of these communities.

In essence, the idea is to devise a multifaceted media strategy to sell achievement, not just to try for a one-shot splash. Now, I'm no advertising executive. Yet it strikes me that the following steps are key:

• Enlist a first-rate advertising firm to devise a multifaceted strategy to market achievement and close the sale in the minds of students and parents.

• Enlist local corporate and media partners (radio, cable, television, and the Internet) that will support and sustain the campaign with financial and in-kind contributions.

• Enlist major community institutions, including churches and PTAs, as well as local women's and men's groups that have sizable memberships and in-house communications vehicles, like bulletins and newsletters in print or via the Web.

• Determine the target audiences, such as schoolchildren of varying ages; leaders of CBOs, businesses, civic and social groups, churches, youth-serving agencies, and PTAs; constituent members of these organizations; station managers and on-air talent at local radio, TV, and cable stations; and local bloggers.

• Decide which messages are likely to be most effective, which ones should be prepared for which audience, what are the most effective means of reaching them and with what frequency, and so on.

• Estimate the cost of producing the messages and implementing the campaign to sell achievement; develop and pursue a fundraising drive to amass cash and in-kind contributions needed to implement the marketing effort.

• Devise an implementation plan, including production timetable, rollout, and follow-through.

• Make provisions to monitor whether and how well the messages are received, whether they change the attitudes and behavior of schoolchildren vis-à-vis reading and achievement, and whether and to what extent students' academic performance is affected.

• Modify the sales campaign as needed or indicated based on how well it rolls out and how target audiences respond.

These ideas are merely suggestive. Experts in marketing, advertising, sales, and media are vastly smarter than I in devising a sales pitch of this kind and determining how it should roll out to maximum effect. The bottom line is that we need to convince young people and their parents to "buy" achievement, using the same kind of creativity and persistence that marketers use to sell consumer goods.

Finding Funding

Those Urban League affiliates that carried out successful events generally had energetic young education coordinators who knew how to organize events and groups and how to get things done. Not surprisingly, an overarching issue from the very beginning was money. Some affiliates viewed the Achievement Campaign as an unfunded mandate imposed by the national office. They didn't have the capacity or inclination to proceed in the absence of new funding up front to support the effort.

The National Urban League did manage to attract national funders, such as State Farm and the Lilly Endowment, which in turn allowed us to allocate funds to many affiliates. This funding enabled us to provide modest grants to some affiliates, which in turn leveraged these resources quite creatively. An enthusiastic national partner in the Achievement Campaign, State Farm supported many of the events, providing modest grants and welcome cachet. It awarded scholarships and other perks to the young people, gave them gift bags and school supplies, and provided local volunteers to help organize and staff the ceremonies.

Securing local sponsorship support posed a different challenge. Typically, the budgets of some of the affiliates and community partners were so tight, and their agendas were so overloaded, that generating the resources needed to implement the events received less attention from them than was necessary. Yet once some of the Urban

League affiliates saw that they could attract financial support from local companies—and then convert these new backers into ongoing supporters of their organization—they appreciated the appeal and potential of the Achievement Campaign.

In most communities, national funding sources will not be in the picture. Therefore, school districts, community groups, and business groups that want to collaborate in staging mobilization events like Achievement Month, the achievement fair, and Achievement Day parades will need to prospect for local sources of funding. As challenging as fund-raising can be, I would venture to speculate that a tight-knit partnership between an enthusiastic school district and committed community groups that are hell-bent on motivating children to learn could prove to be a compelling proposition for local funders. The keys to success in raising funds will be the seriousness of the enterprise, the thoughtfulness of the action plan, the potential impact of the events, the capacity of the steering committee to execute the game plan, its clearheaded grasp of the implementation challenges ahead, and the plans to assess the impact of the effort on the attitudes and academic performance of the children.

As for the actual funding prospects, I would suggest approaching the following:

• *Local community foundations*, which in some regions of the country have ample resources. They generally have two sources for their grants. The first are grants given from unrestricted income derived from their unrestricted endowment. The second category is grants given for activities that must be aligned with the purposes stipulated by the donors of restricted funds to the foundation. Although the latter may sound constrained, oftentimes donors want their funds earmarked to serve educational purposes or to help disadvantaged children. Therefore, grants for a mobilization campaign to motivate youngsters to achieve might qualify even for these more restricted grants.

• *The local chapter of the United Way,* an organization that has become rather proactive and strategic in its grant making in further-ance of community priorities. Education probably ranks high on the totem pole of priorities in the eyes of many United Ways. What's more, a number of the potential community partners in a mobiliza-tion effort, such as social service and youth services agencies, proba-bly already receive support from the United Way. An initiative such as this, in conjunction with the school system, might well strike the United Way as innovative and promising.

• *Local family foundations,* many of which have amassed signifi-cant wealth and support favored priorities and projects of the donors that routinely include education. These foundations often operate well below the radar and might not even have professional staffs. An outfit called the Foundation Center maintains a comprehensive com-puterized database of probably all foundations in the United States, including those that are virtually unknown. The steering committee could mine this database to identify local family foundations that can be approached on behalf of the mobilization effort. With these fam-ilies, it will be important to demonstrate that the effort is aimed at producing a demonstrable and measurable difference in the attitudes and academic performance of youngsters.

• *Local businesses,* many of which have a professed stake in edu-cation because the quality of their workforces hinges on the quality of graduates coming out of local schools. These companies and entrepre-neurs often belong to civic-minded groups like the Chamber of Com-merce, Kiwanis, and Rotary that support education and youth-development initiatives. They are a natural to approach for support, particularly sponsorship of the high-profile events. Also, they often strongly encourage their employees to volunteer in conjunction with causes supported by the business. This can be a valued source of volunteers to help plan and run the various mobilization events.

• *Local branches of national corporations*, which often embrace causes like these mobilization activities. The local branches, which often delight in sponsoring high-profile activities that benefit children, could be asked to provide grants out of their coffers that are matched by the corporation's foundation at headquarters. As was the case with State Farm and other national corporations that supported the Urban League's Achievement Campaign, employees in the local branches can join the army of volunteers who help plan and pull off the individual mobilization events.

• *Public education funds*, which typically support tutorial programs, extracurricular clubs, and other supplemental educational programs aimed at improving the learning experience and boosting the achievement levels of schoolchildren. These groups usually raise their money from local businesses, foundations, and individuals and via fund-raising events. They are a natural partner for the community mobilization initiative.

• *The school system itself*, especially because many districts have received additional funding for boosting student achievement from the federal No Child Left Behind law and from their states by virtue of the school finance equalization lawsuits. If and when school districts become convinced that these community mobilization campaigns actually help bolster student achievement along with the academic performance of individual schools, it would behoove them to "put some skin in the game" because doing so serves their institutional self-interest.

• *State departments of education*, which also invest in improving schools, could be approached for grants to support these efforts, provided, again, that they are thoughtfully conceived and focused on producing measurable improvements in the academic performance of traditionally low-performing students and schools.

• *Designated tax levy support,* as was enacted in Florida to support innovative approaches to improving student outcomes. This rather unusual funding source may be a model worth encouraging, provided the governor, state legislature, or other taxing authority can be persuaded that the investment will pay off in boosting the lowly achievement levels of underperforming students.

The bottom line is that many of these prospective funders care deeply about education. They might be attracted to initiatives like those suggested in this book because of the clear objective and the pro-achievement energy unleashed by these activities.

Sustaining Momentum

The mantra of contemporary school reform is "Close the achievement gap." In actuality, there are gaps aplenty that must be closed: the one between U.S. youngsters and those of other industrialized nations, not to mention surging global competitors like India and China; the gulf that separates low-income and minority students from their economically advantaged peers; and the gap between pupils in inner-city versus suburban schools.

If these academic chasms are to be closed and, more important, if the United States is to be a civil, prosperous, and globally competitive society in the 21st century, then we urgently need all hands on deck. That means educators and policymakers rising for real to the challenge of leaving no child behind. It means parents, as their children's first teachers, shouldering their fair share of responsibility for rearing youngsters who are well adjusted and who come to school in a frame of mind to learn. And it means communities relentlessly setting the value that achievement matters so that children embrace the message in earnest.

To succeed in selling the message that achievement matters, children must be enveloped in a climate of achievement from which there is no escape. As James P. Comer (2004) recalls so poignantly, when he was growing up, all of the adults in his life were locked in a conspiracy to make certain he and his siblings were successful. This culture of achievement worked its wonders organically as well as consciously.

Because the communities where so many chronic underachievers are reared today do not function in remotely the same way as they used to, the existence of these support mechanisms and messages cannot be left to chance. The ideas presented in this book may strike readers as isolated initiatives. But that surely isn't the way I envision them.

The agenda of activities could be drawn from those suggested in this book and from other creative ideas that local groups devise. In addition to coming up with good ideas, it is critically important for educators and community groups to commit to stay the course month in and month out, year in and year out. They should conduct periodic and forthright assessments of how the campaign is faring, make midcourse corrections as needed, and, above all, gauge whether youngsters actually are getting the message that achievement matters. After all, the bottom-line goal is to demonstrate that communities actually can be mobilized to motivate children to achieve.

There could and should be a continuum of activities that encourage, recognize, and reward achievement throughout the school year. This approach creates a drumbeat that resonates from one season to the next and that reaches every school, every classroom, and every community. Imagine a calendar of events roughly along the following lines:

• *September*—Achievement Month rallies and festivals to herald the resumption of school, the dawn of a new opportunity to achieve.

• *October*—Doing the Right Thing assemblies and events in schools, community centers, and churches, all staged on the same day across the community. These events would recognize youngsters who have engaged in a wide array of activities that the community values, from getting better grades the previous year, to successfully completing summer school, to partaking in a community service project.

• *November*—Awards ceremonies for the community groups that did a wonderful job of promoting literacy and achievement during the previous school year.

• *December*—Literacy, math, and/or science fairs and contests that provide incentives for youngsters to display their academic prowess and opportunities to display what they have learned.

• *January*—Induction ceremonies for local community-based honor societies, based on students' academic performance during the first semester.

• *March*—Achievement fairs patterned after county fairs that enable youngsters to explore and demonstrate academically relevant projects of their choosing. There could be a community-wide fair or smaller ones staged on the same day in venues across the community.

• *May*—Achievement Day parades for all 4th and 8th graders who pass the state-mandated examinations in reading and/or math.

• *June*—Second yearly induction ceremony for community-based achiever societies and recognition luncheons for graduating seniors who earned *B* averages or better throughout their high school careers.

A Note of Caution

I would be less than forthright if I did not share the thoughtful perspective of T. Willard Fair, the longtime CEO of the Urban League of Greater Miami who chairs the Florida State Board of Education. A veteran community organizer who cares passionately about improving children's achievement levels and life prospects, he feels it is important to take community mobilization around education beyond celebrations and into the realms of parent responsibility and education policy. He stressed to me that we must create incentives—and disincentives—to spur parents to do what they should do. We must get more mayors involved by using the challenge of closing the achievement gap to get parents and corporations engaged. Policymakers must connect the need to improve schools and student achievement to the economic prosperity of their communities.

In order for community groups to play a prominent leadership and catalytic role, in Fair's view, they must have credibility and authority in the field of education or else they will not be accepted by the community. Having established that reputation in Liberty City, the Miami Urban League created independent parent councils for each school in partnership with a group called Concerned African-American Women. The Urban League also created the Liberty City Service Partnership, a coalition of 20 community-based and faith-based organizations. The consensus among these groups is that low achievement lies at the core of much antisocial behavior in Liberty City.

What's also critically important, Fair cautions, is that this mobilization initiative not be viewed as adversarial vis-à-vis the schools. In Miami, the school district is an active participant in the partnership. The deputy superintendent sits on the overall planning committee, and principals serve on the individual school councils.

For all the benefits, mobilizing communities poses organizational challenges for those groups that assume lead administrative responsibility for the effort. For instance, some Urban League affiliates experienced turnover among staff who, feeling they were paid too little for too much work, left for better-paying, less-demanding jobs. This turnover phenomenon demonstrates the downside of relying on paid staff at community agencies to do the mobilization work. Although depending on volunteers carries risks as well, it's important to minimize the chances of destabilization due to staff defections. In other cases, the absence of leadership at the top made the job of coordinating a campaign particularly burdensome. Understaffing, unstable staffing, and ambivalent leadership can have a negative impact wherever they occur (AED, 2005).

Velma Cobb, who directs the Achievement Campaign for the National Urban League, adds yet another dose of reality by admitting that it can be a struggle for community-based organizations involved in advocacy and direct services to stay the course because they are constantly pulled in so many different directions depending on the needs of those they serve. Convincing leaders and designated staff of groups like these to stay on track is critically important.

She noted to me that one useful way to do this is by giving them how-to materials—handbooks, prototypes of letters, suggested procedures and timetables, and so forth—that spell out what, how, and when they should implement the activities. Resourceful community-based organizations and their partners can then take it from there. In conjunction with the National Achievers Society, for instance, Cobb produced guidebooks, prototype letters, templates, and standardized procedures, which helped local sponsors who were strapped for time and resources to implement the routine aspects of NAS without hampering their creativity.

If the metaphor of the village is to resonate vibrantly in contemporary society, its principal and most urgent manifestation rests in rallying around the education and healthy development of the children who are, after all, America's destiny. The education challenges facing our country in the 21st century exceed the capacity of schools and educators to solve on their own. Communities can be mobilized to motivate children to achieve. They have successfully been mobilized to motivate youngsters to achieve. If the persistent achievement gaps holding back American children, and thus the United States, are to be closed, then communities must be mobilized to motivate their youngsters to achieve. Inertia is not an option.

Real-world experience with the Urban League's Achievement Campaign vividly illustrates the impressive rewards and readily manageable risks of mobilizing communities to motivate children to achieve. To repeat the main point of this book, it can be done because it has been done. Youngsters will respond if only the adults in the village will bestir themselves to inspire them.

Ways to Get the Ball Rolling

- Take the initiative and demonstrate your commitment to partner with community groups.
- Select community partners that genuinely care about children and have a track record of delivering on their promises and staying the course.
- Forge a consensus on the need for a school/community alliance to motivate youngsters to achieve.

- Establish a joint steering committee to spearhead the mobilization, select the key activities, and determine the implementation timetable.
- Seek and secure funding for core staffing and operating costs for the partnership and its activities.
- Encourage community partners to devise their own motivational ideas and incorporate these into the agenda.
- Launch a first initiative, take stock, and press forward with a year-round, multiyear strategy.

CONCLUDING THOUGHTS

When I headed the National Urban League, the organization's slogan was "Our Children = Our Destiny." Why this rallying cry? The rationale could not be simpler. Children may be just a portion of a nation's population, but they are 100 percent of its future.

Many youngsters already achieve at high levels and receive appropriate doses of support, encouragement, and guidance from their parents and communities. Yet the stark reality is that millions of American children are marginalized academically and thus destined for social and economic oblivion in the 21st century. They will not be able to uphold their obligations as citizens and providers. Their plight stems from many factors, including family, neighborhood, and economic circumstances beyond their control. Some youngsters are so intimidated by their classmates that they do not even strive to do well in school. Still other youngsters seem indifferent to achievement and disenchanted with formal education as they've known it.

In noted school reformer James P. Comer's poignant observation about the black American experience—an observation I believe applies to other groups on the margins of America's mainstream—modernity has weakened the role of families and communities when it comes to inculcating achievement values in children: "Many of today's students at greatest risk for underachievement or school failure are growing up in families that did not experience three generations of acculturation and upward mobility" (2004, p. 89). According to Comer, "The application of science and technology to most aspects of life simultaneously created forces that make it much more difficult for families and communities to adequately support the development of children" (pp. 82–83).

ASCD's Commission on the Whole Child emerged from its assignment utterly convinced that it will be impossible to close those nagging achievement gaps and get all of America's children on course for successful and productive adulthoods unless we take a more holistic look at what's happening in the lives of children. *The Learning Compact Redefined* (2007), the report issued by the Commission, makes the case eloquently and points the way strategically. For the sake of the schools and the schoolchildren, local educators and community leaders in particular need to team up to neutralize and, yes, defeat the forces that thwart the inclination and ability of youngsters to achieve.

Back in the 1800s, homesteading gave the poorest in society a big lift by giving them 40 acres and a mule. We urgently need the 21st-century equivalent of homesteading for America's children who are performing below par and lagging behind in school. In other words, in today's so-called knowledge economy, we need what one economics writer wryly calls "40 acres and a sheepskin" (Goozner, 2002). By teaming up, local educators and community leaders can forge a potent, positive conspiracy to help our children to strive for success in school and ultimately in life.

REFERENCES

Academy for Educational Development. (2005, February). *Campaign for African American achievement phase I 10/99–10/04 evaluation.* Prepared for the National Urban League. Washington, DC: Author.

Aronson, J. M. (Ed.). (2002). *Improving academic achievement: Impact of psychological factors on education.* New York: Academic Press.

Association for Supervision and Curriculum Development. (2007). *The learning compact redefined: A call to action; A report of the Commission on the Whole Child.* Alexandria, VA: Author.

Balfanz, R., & Legters, N. (2006, July 12). Closing dropout factories. *Education Week, 25*(42), pp. 42–43.

Bing, L. (1989, March). When you're a Crip (or a Blood): Forum. *Harper's,* 51–59.

Brown, D. (1996, September 20). Urban League lauds youth progress. *Morning Journal* (Cleveland, OH).

Center for Strategic and International Studies. (2000). *American military culture in the twenty-first century.* Washington, DC: CSIS International Security Program, Center for Strategic and International Studies.

Chandler, M. A. (2007, February 20). Black parents seek to raise ambitions. *Washington Post,* p. A1.

Coleman, J. S. (1988). Social capital in the creation of human capital. *American Journal of Sociology, 94* (Supplement, "Organizations and institutions: Sociological and economic approaches to the analysis of social structure").

Comer, J. P. (2004). *Leave no child behind: Preparing today's youth for tomorrow's world.* New Haven, CT: Yale University Press.

Cullinan, M., Eaves, J. K., McCurdy, D., & McCain, J. (1992). *Forging a military youth corps: A military–youth service partnership for high school dropouts.* Final report of the CSIS National Community Service for Out-of-School Youth Project. Boulder, CO: Westview.

Daniels, L. (1997, September 21). League march honors youth success. *Sunday Oregonian.*

DeNeal, L. (1997, September 25). Education parade receives high marks. *Post-Tribune* (Gary, IN), p. NB3.

DeNeal, L. (1998, March 20). 500 from 3 counties honored. *Post-Tribune* (Gary, IN), p. B3.

DeNeal, L. (2000, September 17). Day ideal for ACCORD parade. *Post-Tribune* (Gary, IN).

Dillon, S. (2007, June 1). U.S. data show rapid minority growth in school rolls. *New York Times*, p. A21. Retrieved December 12, 2007, from http://www.nytimes.com/2007/06/01/education/01educ.html

Diplomas count: An essential guide to graduation policy and rates. (2006, June 22). *Education Week*, 25(41), p. 7.

Dweck, C. S. (2002). Messages that motivate: How praise molds students' beliefs, motivation, and performance (in surprising ways). In J. M. Aronson (Ed.), *Improving academic achievement: Impact of psychological factors on education* (pp. 37–60). New York: Academic Press.

Eisenberg, J. (1996, June 17). Luncheon honors black scholars. *The Journal News* (Westchester County, NY), p. 8.

Fisher, E. J. (2005, Summer). Black student achievement and the oppositional culture model. *Journal of Negro Education*, 74(3), 201.

Flanagan, A., & Grissmer, D. (2002). The role of federal resources in closing the achievement gap. In J. Chubb & T. Loveless (Eds.), *Bridging the achievement gap* (pp. 199–226). Washington, DC: Brookings Institution.

Ford, D. Y., & Harris, J. J., III. (1996, June). Perceptions and attitudes of black students toward school, achievement, and other educational variables. *Child Development*, 67(3), 1141–1152.

Gewertz, C. (2006, March 8). H.S. dropouts say lack of motivation top reason to quit. *Education Week*, 25(26), p. 14.

Goodenow, C. (1993, February). Classroom belonging among early adolescent students: Relationships to motivation and achievement. *Journal of Early Adolescence*, 13(1), 37.

Goozner, M. (2002, November 30). Forty acres and a sheepskin. *American Prospect*. Retrieved December 12, 2007, from http://www.prospect.org/cs/articles?article=forty_acres_and_a_sheepskin

Harris Interactive. (2005). *Values of scouts: A study of ethics and character*. Irving, TX: Boy Scouts of America Youth and Family Research Center. Available: http://www.scouting.org/media/research/02-882.pdf

Hayes, L. (2001, September 15). Students celebrate education. *Cincinnati Enquirer*. Retrieved December 12, 2007, from http://www.enquirer.com/editions/2001/09/15/loc_students_celebrate.html

Haynes, V. D. (1996, October 19). D.C. study sees bleak rate for college graduation. *Washington Post*, p. B1.

Hill, N. E., Castellino, D. R., Lansford, J. E., Nowlin, P., Dodge, K. A., Bates, J. E., & Petit, G. S. (2004, September–October). Parent academic involvement as related to school behavior, achievement, and aspirations: Demographic variations across adolescence. *Child Development*, 75(5), 1491–1509.

Honoring student achievement. (2004, May). *Education Digest*, p. 27. Available: www.eddigest.com

Katz, A. (2002, January 31). Charter school stresses academics, discipline. *Alameda Times-Star* (Alameda, CA), p. 1.

Kolb, C. (2006, July 12). The cracks in our education pipeline. *Education Week*, *25*(42), 45, 56.

Kunjufu, J. (1988). *To be popular or smart: The black peer group*. Chicago: African American Images.

Kyriakos, M. (1996, May 1). Recognition for all sorts of class acts: D.C. students receive "right thing" acclaim. *Washington Post*, p. D3.

Labbé, T. (2007, June 14). Students celebrate as college dreams come step closer. *Washington Post*, District Extra, p. DZ01, 8.

LeGrier, R. (1997, September 24). Hundreds close ranks at the state capitol in celebration of youth "doing the right thing." *Hartford Inquirer* (Hartford, CT) p. 1.

Lewin, T. (2006, September 7). Report finds U.S. students lagging in finishing college. *New York Times*, p. A23. Retrieved December 12, 2007, from http://www.nytimes.com/2006/09/07/education/07educ.html?_r=1&oref=slogin

Loveless, T. (2006). How well are American students learning? *The 2006 Brown Center report on American education*, *II*(1). Washington, DC: Brookings Institution.

March, book fair celebrate what's right about youth. (1997, September 4). *Oregonian*.

March set to promote youth who "do the right thing." (1997, September 3). *The Skanner* (Portland, OR).

McCarthy, G. (2003, September 27). Pulled up by the boot straps: A new Perris school reflects the trend of tackling educational challenges with military-style discipline. *Press Enterprise* (Riverside, CA), p. A1.

Mickelson, R. A. (1990, January). The attitude–achievement paradox among black adolescents. *Sociology of Education*, *63*, 59.

Mishel, L. (2006, March 8). The exaggerated dropout crisis. *Education Week*, *25*(26), p. 40.

Mount Vernon City School District. (2006). *Great schools: The parents' guide to K–12 success*. Retrieved November 2006 from http://www.greatschools.net/cgi-bin/ny/district_profile/423

The Mount Vernon story: A how-to primer for saving our children. (2001, October 18–24). *New York Amsterdam News*.

National Assessment Governing Board. (n.d.). NAEP: Achievement levels. Available: http://nagb.org

National Urban League honors students for academic excellence through induction into National Achievers Society. (2001, July 5). *San Diego Voice & Viewpoint*.

Ogbu, J. U. (1992, November). Understanding cultural diversity and learning. *Educational Researcher*, *21*(8), 5–14.

Olson, L. (2006, January 5). A decade of effort. *Education Week*, *25*(17), pp. 9–10.

Parker, E. L. (2001, April). Hungry for honor. *Interpretation: A Journal of Bible and Theology*, *55*(2), 148.

Parker, K. (1997, September 20). Urban League honors students. *Tampa Tribune*, p. 1.

Paul, L. (1998, September 17). Parade set for takeoff Saturday. *Post-Tribune* (Gary, IN).

Petrick, J. (1997, September 19). Celebrating the good that today's youth do. *Jersey Journal*, p. A5.

Poindexter, G. (2001, October 25–31). Black males make academic excellence "normal": Educating Black Americans, Part III. *New York Amsterdam News*, pp. 6, 38.

Porter, M. K. (1997). The Bauer County Fair: Community celebration as context for youth experiences of learning and belonging. In G. D. Spindler (Ed.),

Education and cultural process: Anthropological approaches (3rd ed.). Prospect Heights, IL: Waveland.

Preckel, F., Holling, H., & Vock, M. (2006). Academic underachievement: Relationship with cognitive motivation, achievement motivation, and conscientiousness. *Psychology in the Schools, 43*(3), 403.

Price, H. B. (1998, November 5). Is somebody watching? *Centre View* (Centreville, VA).

Price, H. B. (2002). *Achievement matters: Getting your child the best education possible.* New York: Kensington Books.

Price, H. B. (2007, May). *Demilitarizing what the Pentagon knows about developing young people: A new paradigm for educating adolescents who are struggling in school and in life.* Washington, DC: Brookings Institution. Available: http://www.brookings.edu/papers/2007/05defense_price.aspx

Puente, M. (1997, September 21). Gary youth celebrate education. *Post-Tribune* (Gary, IN).

Rosenberg, S. L. (1999, September). The need to belong. *American School Board Journal, 186*(9), 26–28.

Ross, R. (2001, July 31). Mt. Vernon, New York School District: A model for effective reform. Presentation at National Urban League Annual Conference, Plenary Session VI.

Rully, D. (1997, September 25–October 1). Closing Ranks II ceremony celebrates youth. *Hartford News* (Hartford, CT), p. 13.

Santana, R., Jr. (2000, September 17). A celebration of promising futures. *San Diego Union-Tribune*, p. B2.

Schultz, G. F. (1993). Socioeconomic advantage and achievement motivation: Important mediators of academic performance in minority children in urban schools. *Urban Review, 25*(3), 228.

Shepard, P. (1998, April 24). Achievement program demands excellence from black youths. Retrieved December 12, 2007, from http://archive.southcoasttoday.com/daily/04-98/04-26-98/a06wn032.htm

Simmons, T. (2001, April 7). Students become high society. *News and Observer* (Raleigh, NC), p. 1B.

Steele, C. M. (1992, April). Race and the schooling of black Americans. *Atlantic Monthly.* Retrieved December 12, 2007, from http://www.theatlantic.com/doc/199204/race-education

Students get push to stay the course. (1997, September 20). Unidentified Puget Sound newspaper, Young Adults Page.

Suskind, R. (1994, May 26). Against all odds: In rough city school, top students struggle to learn—and escape. *Wall Street Journal.* Retrieved December 12, 2007, from http://www.ronsuskind.com/articles/000034.html

Symonds, W. C. (2005, November 21). America the uneducated. *Business Week*, p. 120.

Thomas-Lynn, F. (2006, November 18). League helps students to embrace achievement. *Milwaukee Journal Sentinel.* Retrieved December 12, 2007, from http://www.jsonline.com/story/index.aspx?id=532652

Tough, P. (2006, November 26). What it takes to make a student. *New York Times Magazine.* Retrieved December 12, 2007, from http://www.nytimes.com/2006/11/26/magazine/26tough.html

Venable, S. F. (1997, May). Adolescent rites of passage: An experiential model. *Journal of Experiential Education, 20*(1), 6–13.

Wilson, D. M. (2000, November 24). Students can read their way to bikes. *Journal News* (White Plains, NY), p. 1A.

Zernike, K. (2001, May 23). In 2 years, Mt. Vernon test scores turn around. *New York Times*. Retrieved December 12, 2007, http://query.nytimes.com/gst/fullpage.html?res=9C06E6D6123DF930A15756C0A9679C8B63&n=Top/Reference/Times%20Topics/Subjects/R/Reading%20and%20Writing%20Skills

INDEX

Page numbers followed by *f* indicate a figure.

academic achievement
    community role in, 5, 19–21,
        127–128
    marginalized students and,
        127–128
    personal factors contributing to,
        24–25
    promotion of. *See* literacy
        promotion; National Achievers
        Society; SAT awareness rally
    recognition of. *See* celebrations
    student motivation and, 24–26,
        29–30
Academic Bowl Game, 84
academic competence, NAEP levels of,
    7–8
achievement
    altered sense of, 87
    student. *See* student achievement
Achievement Campaign
    basic strategies of, 46
    community-based honor societies.
        See National Achievers Society
    Doing the Right Thing events,
        59–63
    evaluation of, 22, 64, 86–89
    launch of, 45–47
    literacy promotion. *See* literacy
        promotion

Achievement Campaign *(continued)*
    recognition of student
        accomplishment. *See*
        celebrations
    SAT awareness rally, 74–76
achievement fairs, 51–54
achievement gap, 1, 7–8, 9*f*, 23, 120
*Achievement Matters: Getting Your Child
    the Best Education Possible* (Price),
    5, 15
Achievement Month, 47–49, 87
adaptability, need for, 99
adolescents
    rites of passage and, 39–42
    transition to adulthood,
        32–33
adults, proportion with college
    degrees, 12
Advanced Level of academic
    competence, 8
advertising. *See* media coverage
advertising firm, hiring of, 114
African American books, 69, 70
African American students. *See* black
    students
after-school programs, 21
allegiance to peers, 26–27
American Indian students, ratio of low
    achievers, 8

Association for Supervision and
   Curriculum Development (ASCD),
   6, 128

Balfanz, Robert, 10
Basic Level of academic competence, 7
Bauer County Fair, 52
Bayardelle, Eddy, 11
behavior incentives, 59–63
belief-changing interventions, 29–30
Believers groups, 78, 88
belonging, need for, 26–27, 35–38
Below Basic Level of academic
   competence, 8
bikes, fifty books and, 70–73
billboards, 109–110
Black Scholars Recognition Reception,
   54–57
black students
   achievement gap and, 1, 8, 12
   college preparation of, 8, 10
   community campaign and, 44–47
   community norms, and
      achievement of, 19–21
   dropout rates of, 10
   perceptions of opportunity and
      obstacles by, 26
   ratio of low achievers, 8
   SAT exam and, 74–76
   stigma, and motivation of, 30–31
book fairs, 59–60
books. See literacy promotion
Bowen, Dan, 58, 82
Boy Scouts, 37, 39
businesses, local, 118–119. See also
   corporations

calendar of events, 122
Campaign for African-American
   Achievement. See Achievement
   Campaign.
Canada, Geoffrey, 20
CBOs (community-based
   organizations), 17
celebrations
   achievement fairs, 51–54
   Achievement Month, 47–49, 87
   evaluation of, 64

celebrations (continued)
   good behavior rewards, 59–63
   luncheons and receptions, 54–59
   parades, 49–51
celebrity support, 109
Center for Strategic and International
   Studies (CSIS), 28
ceremonies. See celebrations
Chicago Military Academy, 29, 34
child-centered focus, maintaining,
   102–103
church-based culture, blacks and,
   19–20
churches
   collaboration with, 97–98
   as inner community, 103–104
   mandates and operating principles
      of, 105
   recruitment of, 94
Circle of Life (Matthiessen), 40
Cobb, Velma, 94, 124
Coleman, James, 18
collaborators. See partners
college
   application assistance for, 74–76
   completion rates for, 11–12
   preparation for, 8, 10
college degrees, proportion of adults
   with, 12
Comer, James P., 16, 19–20, 21, 121,
   127–128
Commission on the Whole Child,
   6, 128
committees, 92–94, 102
communication with partners,
   105–106
communities. See also community
   mobilization
   black American, 19–21
   definition of, 17
   in motivation of students, 15,
      17, 23
   norms of, 18–19
   resources potentially provided
      by, 6
   role in fostering academic
      achievement, 5, 19–21, 127–128
   unleashing energy of, 21–22

community-based honor societies.
  See McKnight Achievers Society;
  National Achievers Society
community-based organizations
  (CBOs), 17
community leaders, role of, 94
community mentoring, 21
community mobilization, 90–126
  adaptability and, 99
  campaign launch, 44–47
  challenges, 123–125
  churches as partners, 94, 97–98,
    103–104, 105
  committees and teams, 92–94, 102
  corporations as partners, 98–99,
    105, 106, 119
  educators and, 21–22, 44, 95–96
  financial limitations, 103
  funding, 82–83, 116–120
  getting the ball rolling, 90–95,
    125–126
  local action requirement, 100
  long-term planning, 100
  maintaining focus, 102–103
  objectives for, 99–100
  partnership challenges, 104–106
  publicity. *See* media coverage
  recognition of volunteers, 106–108
  relationships and personal
    contacts in, 101
  student participation, 79, 84–85,
    102
  sustaining momentum, 120–122
  Urban League involvement in, 4,
    33, 44–45
  volunteer groups as partners,
    96–97, 99–100, 106–108
community organization recruitment,
  94. *See also* volunteer groups
confidence, and academic success, 25
Congress of National Black Churches,
  78
conscientiousness, and academic
  success, 25
Cooper, Maudine R., 60
corporate partners
  active involvement of, 99, 106
  collaboration with, 98–99

corporate partners *(continued)*
  mandates and operating principles
    of, 105
  national, 119
cosponsors, 62–63
county fairs, 51–52
CSIS (Center for Strategic and
  International Studies), 28
cultures, rites of passage in, 39, 40
Curry, Lavin, 34–35

DC Achievers program, 58–59
designated tax levy support, 120
devaluation of students, 30–31, 33–34
direct service programs, 45
discipline, and motivation, 28–29
discouragement of children by parents,
  31–32
disengagement crisis, 11, 23
disidentification, 30–31
Doing the Right Thing events, 59–63,
  64, 87
dropout crisis, 10–11, 23
dropout factories, 10
dropping out, reasons cited for, 11

early childhood language exposure,
  intellectual development and, 31–32
educational value of fairs, 52
education departments, funding from,
  119–120
education initiatives, 4, 12–14
Education Summit, 48–49
educators
  in mobilizing community
    involvement, 21–22, 44
  recruiting of, 95–96
Elizabeth Wesley Youth Merit Incentive
  Award Program Luncheon, 57–58
events calendar, 122

Fair, T. Willard, 123
fairs, 51–54, 59–60
faith-based groups. *See* churches
family foundations, 118
family role in fostering academic
  achievement, 16, 31–32, 127–128
federal education initiatives, 12–13

fifty books and a bike, 70–73
financial limitations, 103. *See also*
    funding
flexibility, need for, 99
focus, maintaining, 102–103
Forging a Military Youth Corps: A
    Military–Youth Service Partnership for
    High School Dropouts (CSIS), 28
Foundation Center, 118
foundations, 117–118
4-H Clubs, 39
funding, 82–83, 103, 116–120

galas, 106–108
gangs, 32–33, 35–36
Gentry, Eloise, 67, 68
Girl Scouts, 39
goal accomplishment, recognition of,
    38
good behavior rewards, 59–63
Goodson, Phyllis, 29

Hart, Betty, 31, 32
higher education. *See* college
higher education gap, 11–12
high schools, dysfunctional, 10
Hill, Paul Jr., 39
honor, gangs and, 36
A Hope in the Unseen: An American
    Odyssey from the Inner City to the Ivy
    League (Suskind), 3–4
Horne, Eleanor, 74, 75
how-to materials, 124

induction ceremonies, 79–82
initial mobilization meeting, 90–92
inner community, churches as, 103–104
intellectual development, early
    childhood language exposure and,
    31–32
Internet-based networks, 112–113

Jennings, Cedric, 3–4, 33–34

Kolb, Charles, 8

language exposure, intellectual
    development and, 31–32

Latino students, 8, 10, 12
leaflets, 114
The Learning Compact Redefined
    (ASCD), 6, 128
Legters, Nettie, 10
Lewin, Tamar, 12
Lilly Endowment, 82, 116
Literacy Olympiads, 68–70
literacy promotion
    fifty books and a bike, 70–73
    Literacy Olympiads, 68–70
    mass readathons, 66–68
local action requirement, 100
local businesses, 118–119
local education initiatives, 13
local funding sources, 116–120
local sponsorships, 116–117
long-term planning, 100
low-income students, 1, 7, 12, 27
luncheons, 54–59

marketing campaign. *See* media
    coverage
mass readathons, 66–68
mathematics, NAEP results for 4th and
    8th graders, 9*f*
Mathematics Workshop Program,
    30–31
Matthiessen, Peter, 40
McKnight Achievers Society, 77–78, 82
McLawhorn, J. T., 74, 75
McWilson, Jimma, 102–104
media coverage, 108–116
    avenues for, 100–101, 109–110,
        112–114
    Black Scholars Recognition
        Reception, 55–56
    Doing the Right Thing events, 62
    factors in generating, 110–112
    NAS induction ceremonies, 80, 81
    SAT awareness rallies, 75–76
    selling "Achievement Matters,"
        108–110
    steps for, 114–115
media training, 111
meeting, initial, 90–92
mentoring, 21, 68–69
military, rites of passage in, 39

military model for motivation, 28–29, 37
Mills, Richard, 71
minority groups, community norms and, 20–21
minority students. *See also specific minority groups*
   achievement gap and, 1, 7
   factors impacting motivation of, 24–28
   percent of school enrollment, 7
Mishel, Lawrence, 10
Modest, John, 81
motivation. *See also* student motivation
   military model, 28–29, 37
   research on, 24–28

NAEP (National Assessment of Educational Progress), 7–8, 9f
National Achievers Society (NAS), 77–86
   Believers groups, 78, 88
   collaborators, 82–83
   evaluation of, 87–88
   expanded services, 83–84
   funding, 82
   induction ceremonies, 79–82
   launch of, 77, 78–79
   pro-achievement peer groups, 84–86
National Assessment of Educational Progress (NAEP), 7–8, 9f
national corporations, 119
national funding, 116–117
National Honor Society, 77
national organizations, 100, 104, 119
National Urban League. *See also* Achievement Campaign
   history, 1
   in mobilizing community involvement, 4, 22, 44–45
   slogan, 127
NCLB (No Child Left Behind), 12–13
news coverage. *See* media coverage
Nicholson, Elizabeth, 59
Noble, Kelly Price, 84
No Child Left Behind (NCLB), 12–13
nomination processes, 63

nonacademic assistance, 88–89
nonprofit groups, mandates and operating principles of, 105

obstacles, perception of, 26
Olson, Lynn, 14
Olympiads, literacy, 68–70
opportunity, perception of, 26
oppositional cultures, 25–26, 27
organizational challenges, 124
Orr, Dorothy, 58

pamphlets, 114
Parade 4 Education, 49–50
parades, 49–51
parents
   involvement of, 15–17
   responsibility of, 5, 123
   valuation of students and, 31–32
parochial schools, community norms of, 18
Partner Community Organizations, 57
partners
   churches as, 94, 97–98, 103–104, 105
   corporations as, 98–99, 105, 106, 119
   diversity of, 62–63, 82–83
   how-to materials for, 124
   maintaining engagement of, 104–106, 124
   mandates and operating principles of, 105
   recognition of, 106–108
   recruitment of, 94–95
   volunteer groups as, 96–97, 99–100, 106–108
partnerships, challenges of, 104–106
peer groups
   allegiance to, 26–27
   gangs, 32–33, 35–36
   positive, role of, 36–38, 39
   pro-achievement, 84–86
   valuation by, 32–33
personal contacts in schools, 101
personnel turnover, 96, 124
planning subcommittees, 93

postsecondary education. *See* higher
    education
Powell, Colin, 39, 79
preparation gap, 8, 10
press relations course, 111
Prince, Ernest, 54, 56, 57
pro-achievement peer groups, 84–86
Proficient Level of academic
    competence, 7–8
public education funds, 119
publicity. *See* media coverage
public service spots, 109, 111

radio talk shows, 113
rallies, 61–62, 64
readathons, 66–68
reading, NAEP results for 4th and 8th
    graders, 9f
reading skills. *See* literacy promotion
receptions, 54–59
recognition
        events for. *See* celebrations
        motivation and, 38–42
relationships, 101
religions, rites of passage in, 39, 40
religious groups. *See* churches
research on motivation, 24–28
Richardson, Franklyn, 73
Risley, Todd R., 31, 32
rites of passage, 39–42
rituals, 38–42. *See also* celebrations
Rogers, Tee, 36
Ross, Ronald, 71–72, 73

Salute to Scholars, 58
SAT awareness rally, 74–76
school district leaders, role of, 90,
    91–92, 93–94, 123
schools
        Achievement Campaign benefits
            to, 95–96
        as active participants, 123
        atmosphere of belonging in, 37–38
        community norms and, 18–19
        initiatives in, 4, 12–14
        personal contacts in, 101
        personnel changes in, 96

school system, funding from, 119
science fairs, 52–53
self-concept, development of, 18–19
self-discipline, 28–29
Smith, Pat, 59–60
Smith, Quentin P., 50
social capital, community norms as, 18
socioeconomic status, motivation and,
    26
state education departments, funding
    from, 119–120
state education initiatives, 13
State Farm Life Insurance, 64, 74, 82,
    98, 109, 116, 119
Steele, Claude, 30
steering committee, 92–94, 102
student achievement
        altered sense of, 87
        factors contributing to, 24–25
        launching campaign for, 44–47
        marginalized students and,
            127–128
        motivation and, 24–26, 29–30
        recognition of. *See* celebrations
student motivation, 24–43
        belonging and, 26–27, 35–38
        community norms and, 18–19
        essential information on, 43
        lack of, 11
        military model of, 28–29, 37
        need for emphasis on, 15, 24,
            27–28
        recognition rituals and, 38–42
        research on, 24–28
        student achievement and, 24–26,
            29–30
        valuing students and, 30–35
students. *See also* student achievement;
student motivation
        college completion rates, 11–12
        college preparation, 8, 10
        disengagement of, 11, 23
        dropout rates, 10
        ethnic ratios of low achievers, 8
        participation in Achievement
            Campaign, 79, 84–85, 102
        valuing as individuals, 30–35

Suskind, Ron, 2, 3–4, 33, 85

tax levy support, 120
Taylor, Clarence, 33–34
teachers, as positive force in students' lives, 33–35
teams, 102
Treisman, Uri, 30–31
Tribble, Israel (Ike), 77
Tuskegee Airmen, 50

United Way funding, 118

valuing students as individuals, 30–35
village, proverbial, 15
vision of collaboration, 104

volunteer groups
    collaboration with, 96–97, 106–108
    objectives for, 99–100
volunteer recognition, 106–108

Watkins, Gena Davis, 48
white students, ratio of low achievers, 8
Wylie, Dee, 68

Youth Celebration Day, 59–60
youth corps, 37
youth groups, 36–37, 39. See also peer groups

ABOUT THE AUTHOR

Hugh B. Price is a senior fellow at the Brookings Institution, the nation's oldest think tank. He served as president and CEO of the National Urban League from July 1994 through April 2003. During his tenure, he launched the Urban League's historic Campaign for African-American Achievement. During 2006–2007, he cochaired the Commission on the Whole Child, which was established by the Association for Supervision and Curriculum Development.

From 1978 until 1982, Mr. Price was a member of the editorial board of the *New York Times* and frequently wrote editorials about public education. He later became vice president of the Rockefeller Foundation, where he was instrumental in conceiving and initiating the National Commission on Teaching and America's Future, as well as the National Guard Youth ChalleNGe Program, a quasi-military youth corps aimed at turning around the lives of school dropouts.

Mr. Price is the author of *Achievement Matters: Getting Your Child the Best Education Possible* and numerous articles in education periodicals. Readers are invited to contact him at huprice@yahoo.com.

Related ASCD Resources

At the time of publication, the following ASCD resources were available; for the most up-to-date information about ASCD resources, go to www.ascd.org. ASCD stock numbers are noted in parentheses.

Online Products

Understanding Student Motivation by Jenny Smith (ASCD PD Online Course) (#PD05OC52)

Print Products

Activating the Desire to Learn by Bob Sullo (#107009)

The Big Picture: Education Is Everyone's Business by Dennis Littky with Samantha Grabelle (#104438)

Educational Leadership: Educating the Whole Child (Entire issue, May 2007) (#107033)

Education Update: Tapping Parent and Community Support (Entire issue, April 2008) (#108057)

Motivating Students and Teachers in an Era of Standards by Richard Sagor (#103009)

The New Principal's Fieldbook: Strategies for Success by Pam Robbins and Harvey Alvy (#103019)

Videos and DVDs

Educating Everybody's Children, Tape 4: Increasing Interest, Motivation, and Engagement (#400225)

For additional resources, visit us on the World Wide Web (http://www.ascd.org), send an e-mail message to member@ascd.org, call the ASCD Service Center (1-800-933-ASCD or 703-578-9600, then press 2), send a fax to 703-575-5400, or write to Information Services, ASCD, 1703 N. Beauregard St., Alexandria, VA 22311-1714 USA.